Letters, Numbers, and Shapes!

publications

This book is designed to help teachers and parents instruct young children to develop emergent reading and math skills, including fine motor skills, perpetual motor skills, and cognitive learning skills using the following standards:

- **Phonemic Awareness**

- **Phonics**

- **Vocabulary Development**

- **Emergent Writing**

- **Number Sense, Operation, and Relationships**

- **Problem Solving**

- **Simple Geometry**

An Early Childhood Book by
Karen Sevaly

Copyright © 1999
Teacher's Friend, a Scholastic Company.
All rights reserved.
Printed in the U.S.A.

ISBN-13: 978-0-439-50005-0
ISBN-10: 0-439-50005-2

Letters

Each letter of the alphabet is represented by four separate reproducible pages.

Character Page - Cute cartoon characters illustrating the phonemic sounds of each letter can be used as a student color page. Letter cards, in both upper and lower case, are also included. Display the pages around the classroom to help youngsters recognize the letters and indentify the sounds they make. As additional letters are introduced, have youngsters sort and match the upper and lower case letter cards together.

Letter Page - Ask each student to color the large upper and lower case letters prior to tracing the letters on this page. Encourage students to practice writing the letters on their own in the space provided.

Sign Language - Teaching your students to sign the alphabet will give them a tactile method of remembering each letter. Later, they can sign their names and simple words. The large illustrations will help them hold their fingers in the correct positions. Display the sign language pages as you introduce each letter of the alphabet.

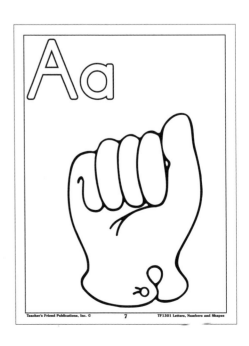

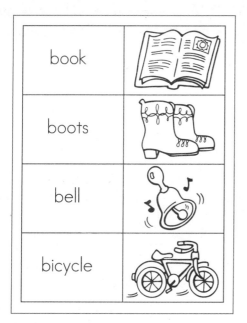

Matching Cards - Four matching word and illustration cards help young children practice the sounds each letter makes. (Cut the cards apart and mount them on squares of poster board. Laminate the cards for durability.) Young learners will begin to recognize the specific words while matching the cards. As additional letters and sounds are learned, more cards can be added to the matching activity.

Student-Made Letter Posters - Young children can make simple posters for each letter of the alphabet. Have the children color and cut out the pages for each specific letter. The elements can be arranged and pasted to a large sheet of construction paper. As each letter is introduced and mastered, have your students make the posters and take them home to share with parents.

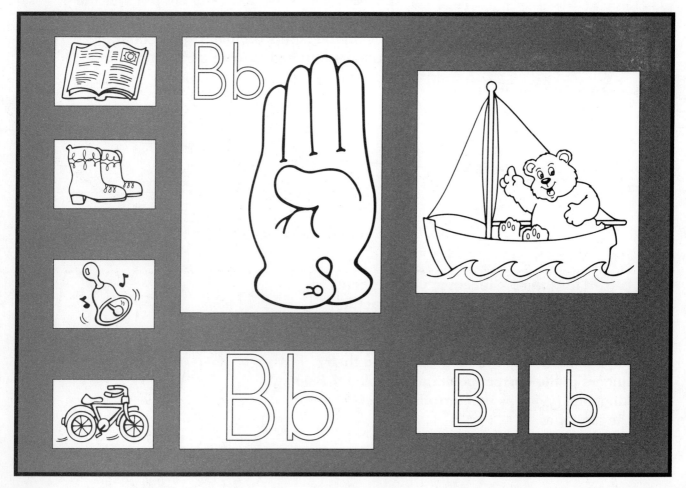

ape
apple

A a

TF1301 Letters, Numbers and Shapes

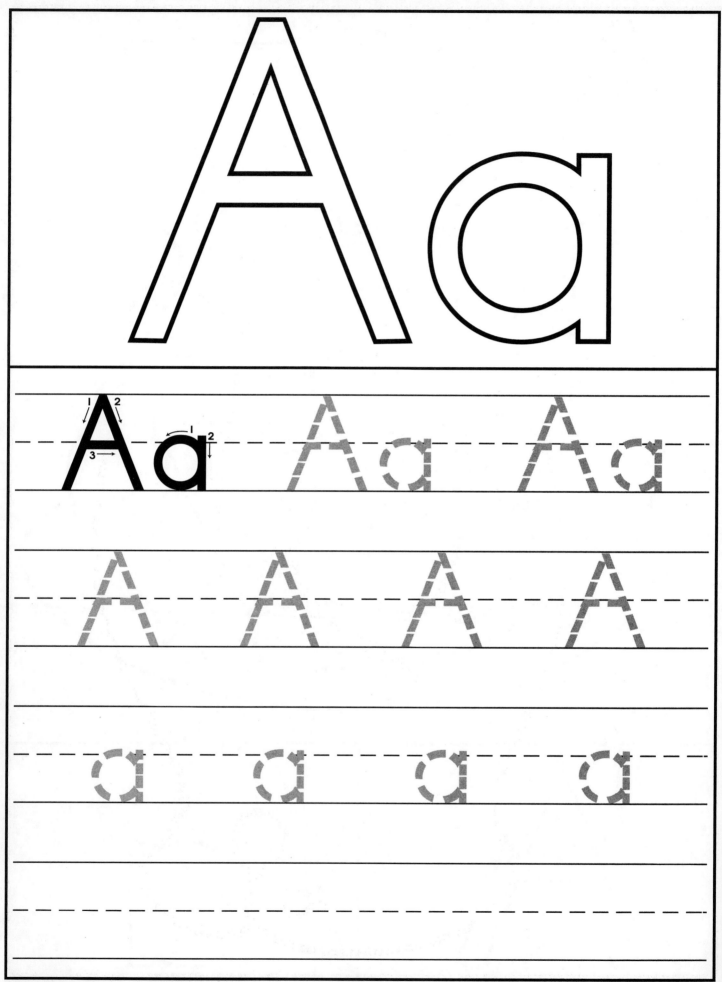

Aa

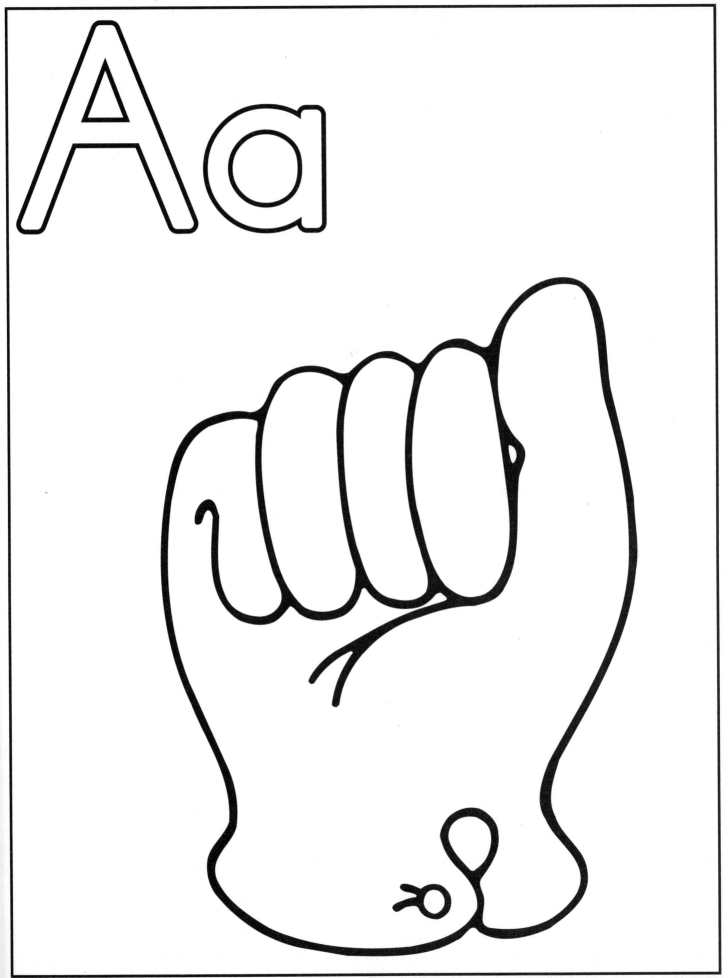

apple	
angel	
alligator	
anchor	

bear
boat

B   b

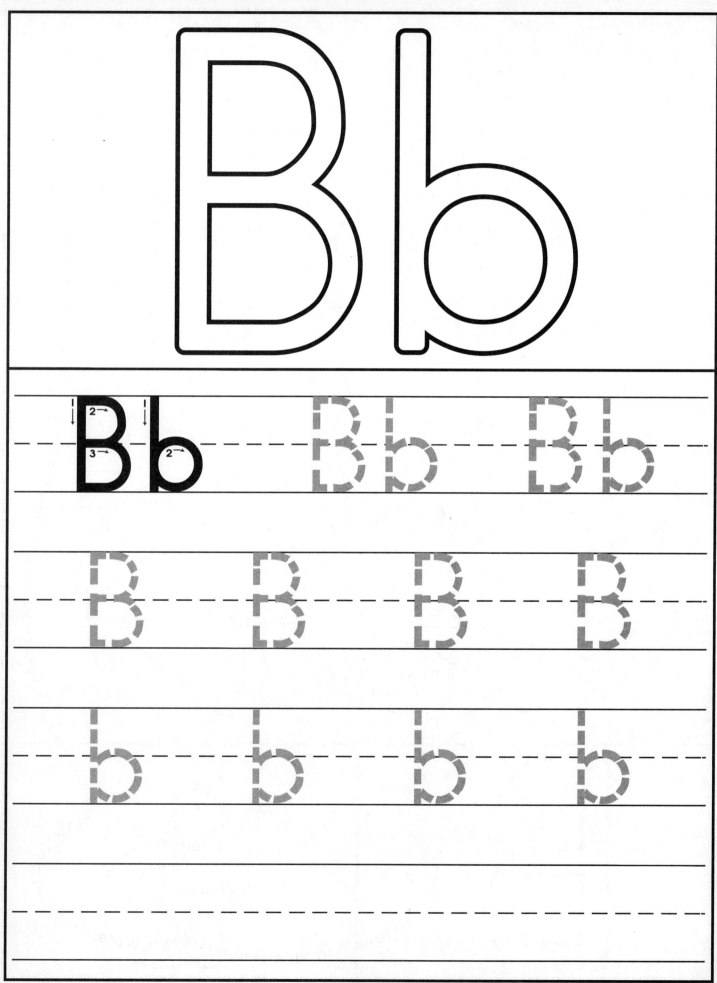

book	
boots	
bell	
bicycle	

cat
candle

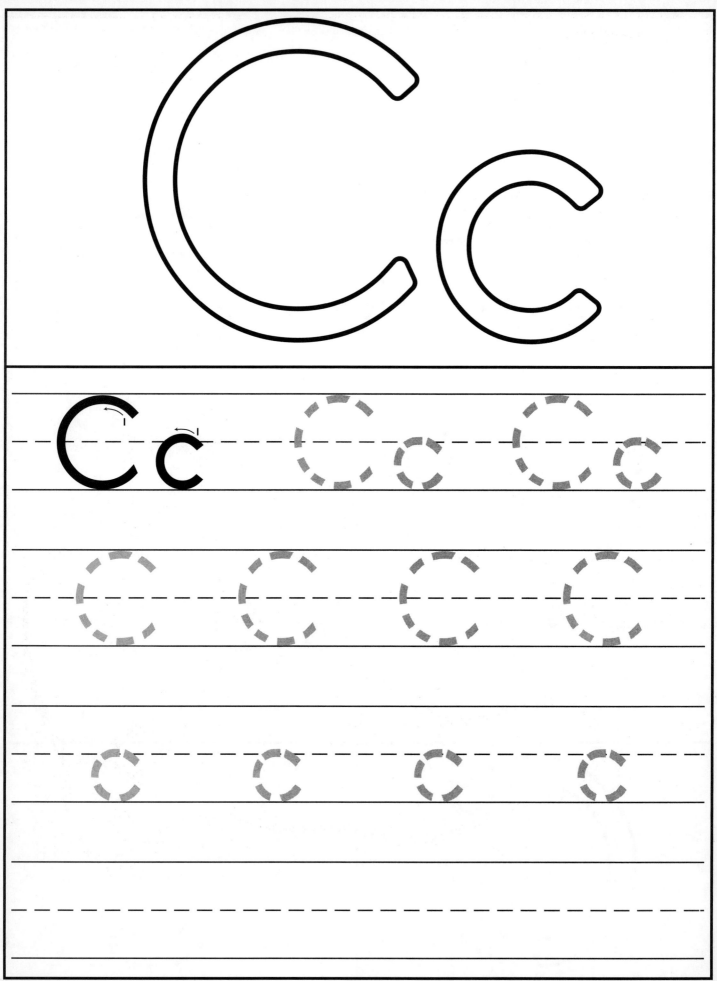

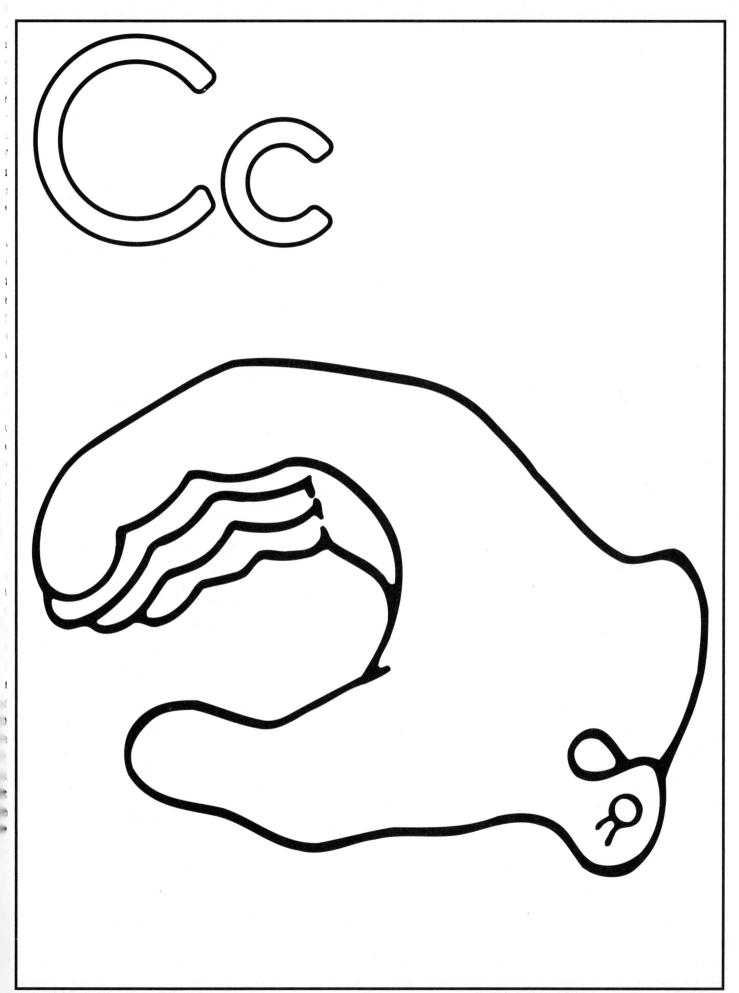

car	
cup	
cow	
candle	

dinosaur
doughnut

D

d

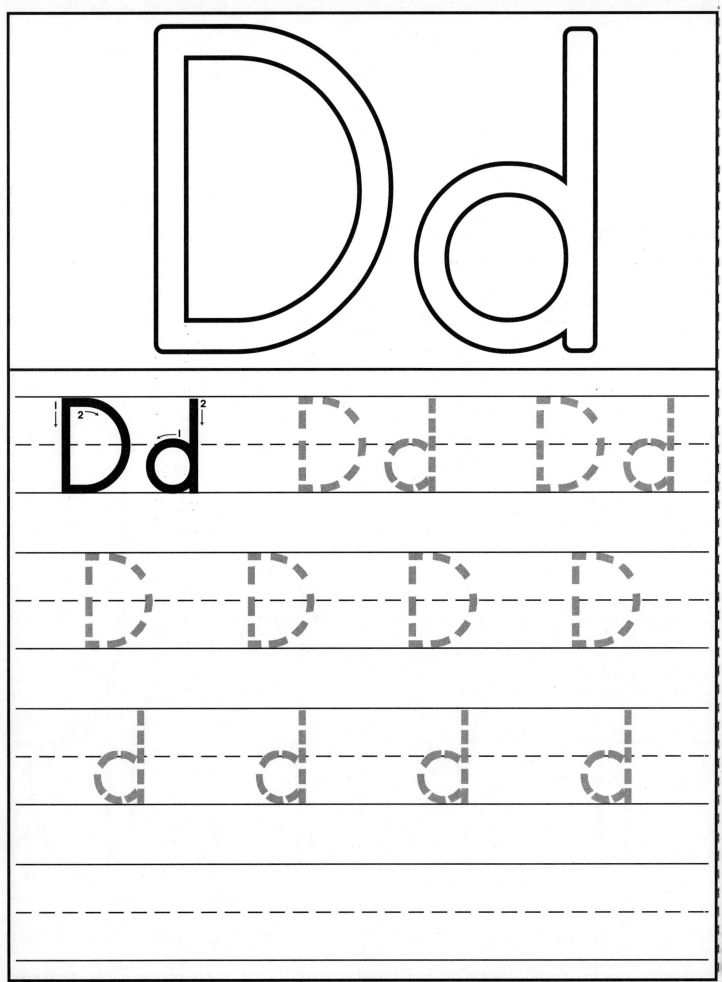

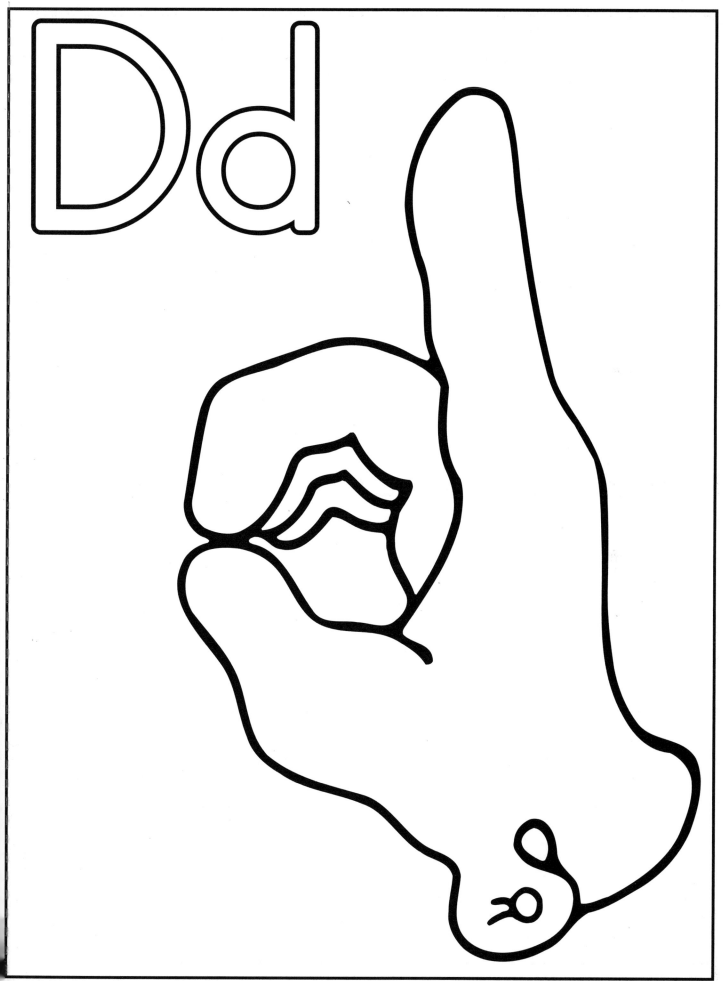

duck	
dog	
door	
dinosaur	

egg
elephant

E

e

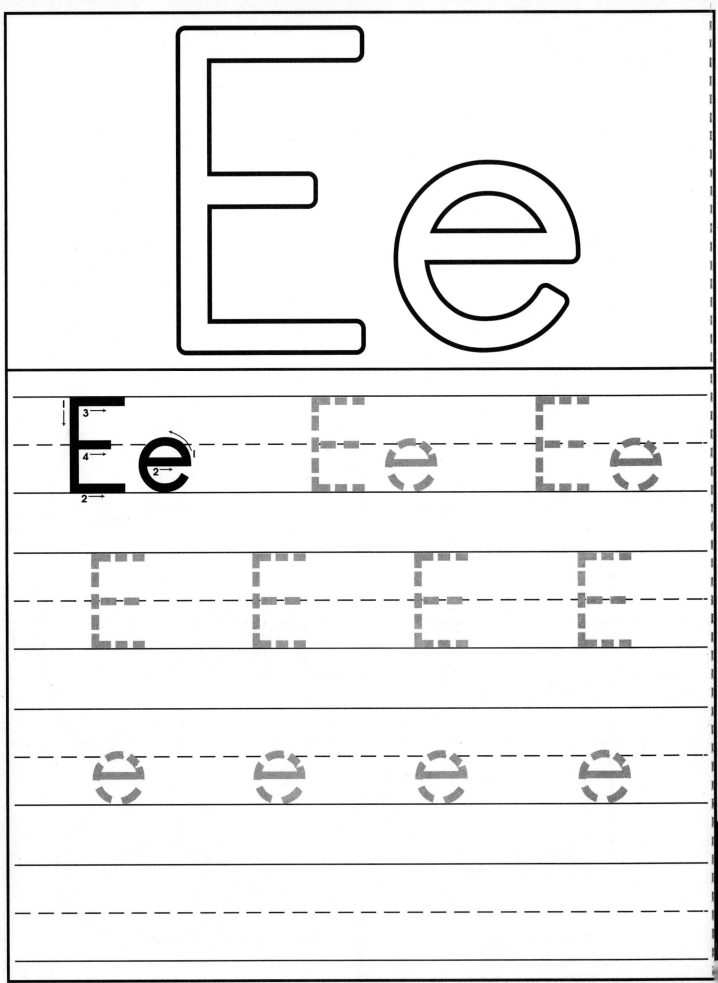

Ee

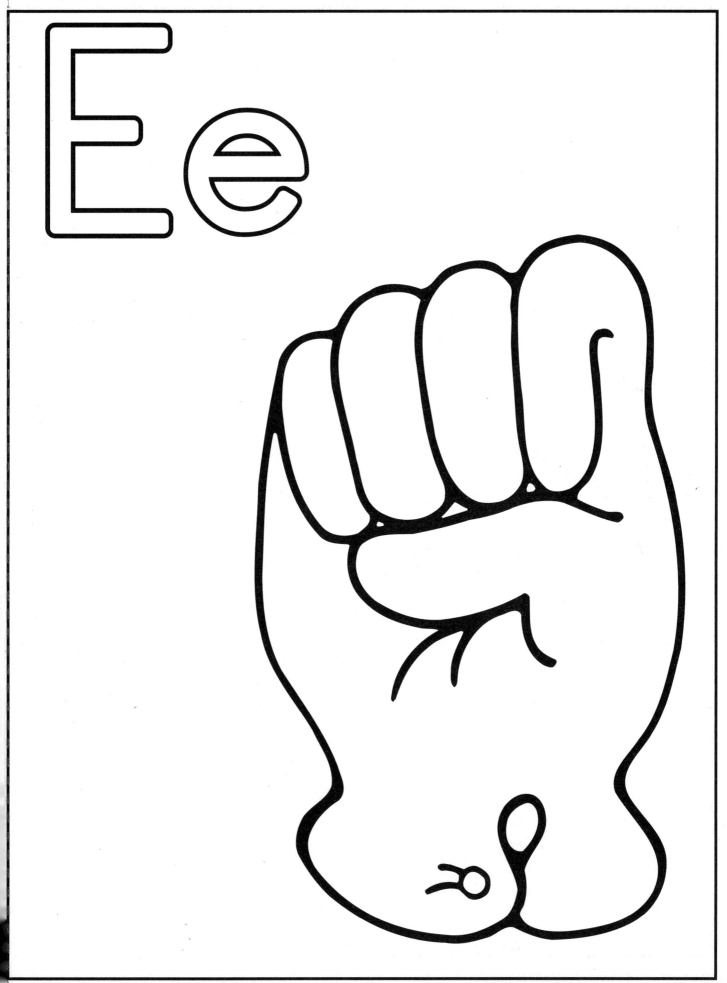

elephant	
eagle	
egg	
envelope	

fan
fish

F

f

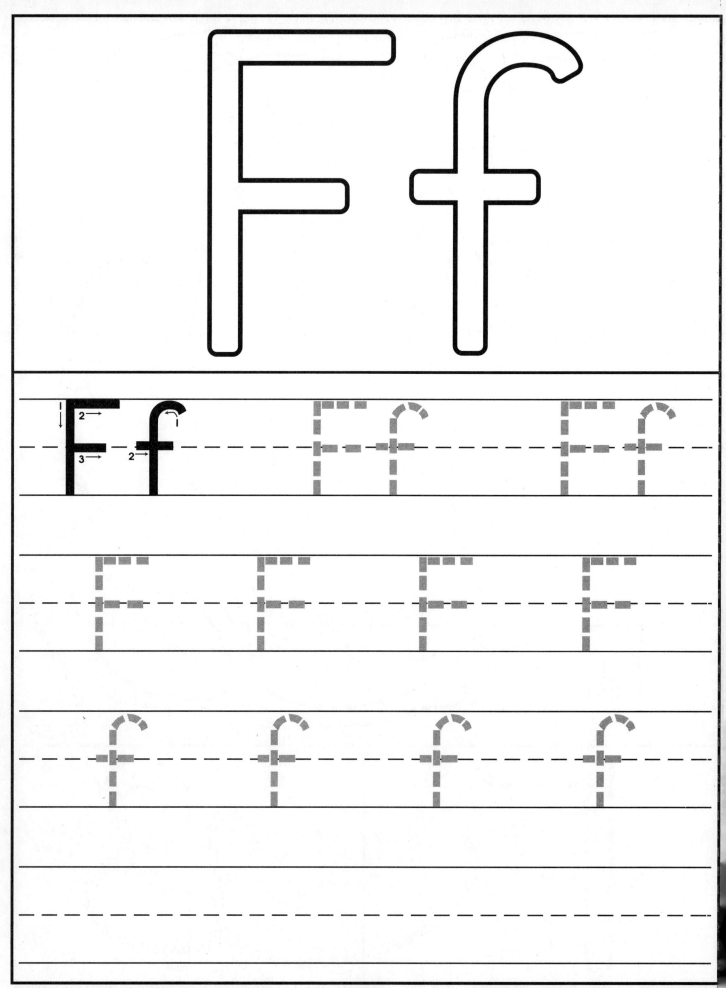

F f

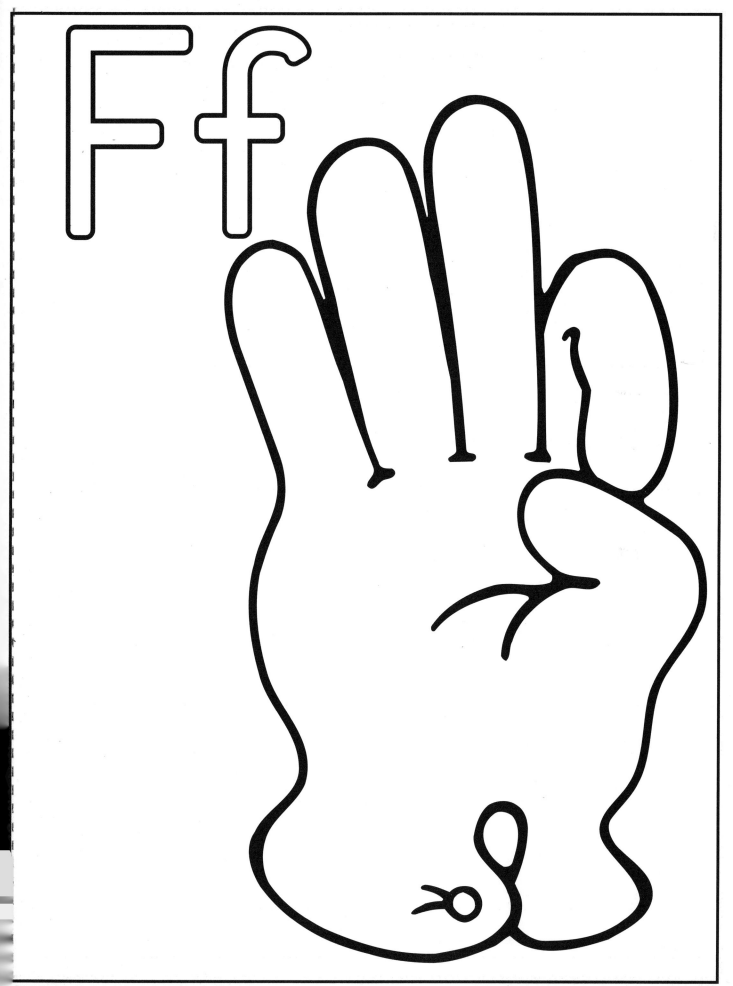

27

fox	
fork	
fish	
fan	

goose
guitar

G

g

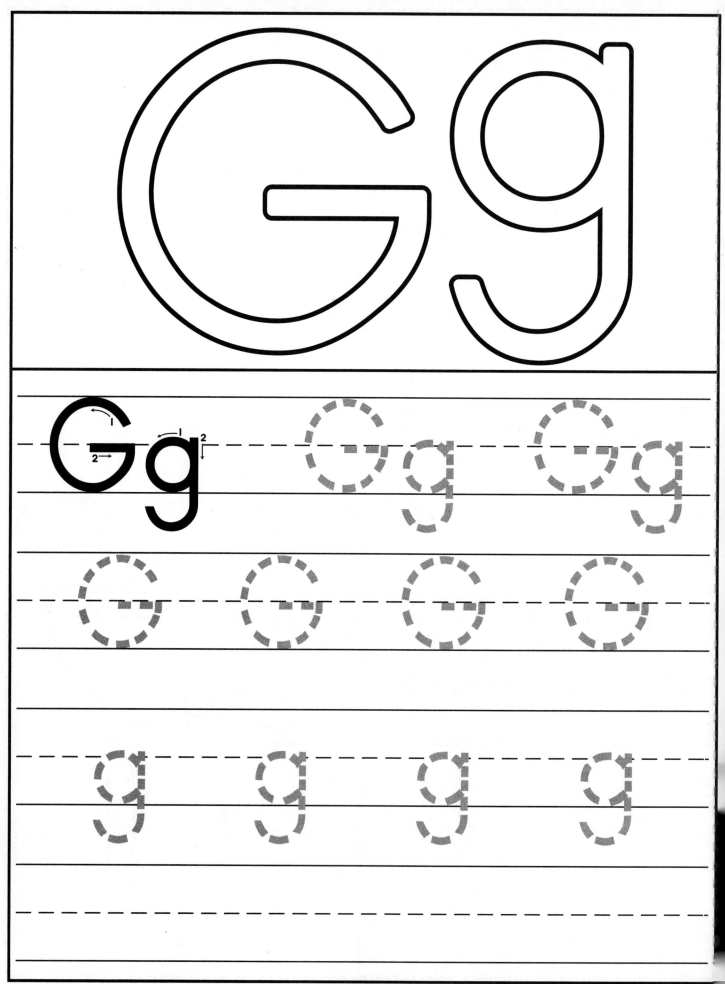

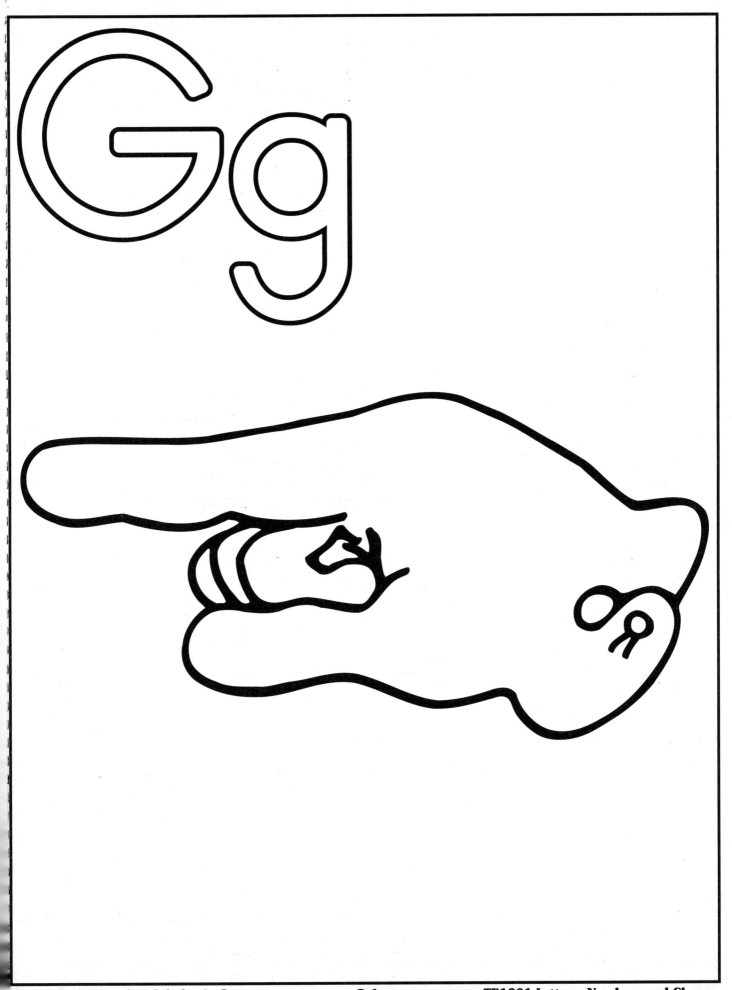

goat	
guitar	
ghost	
gate	

hippopotamus
hat

H   h

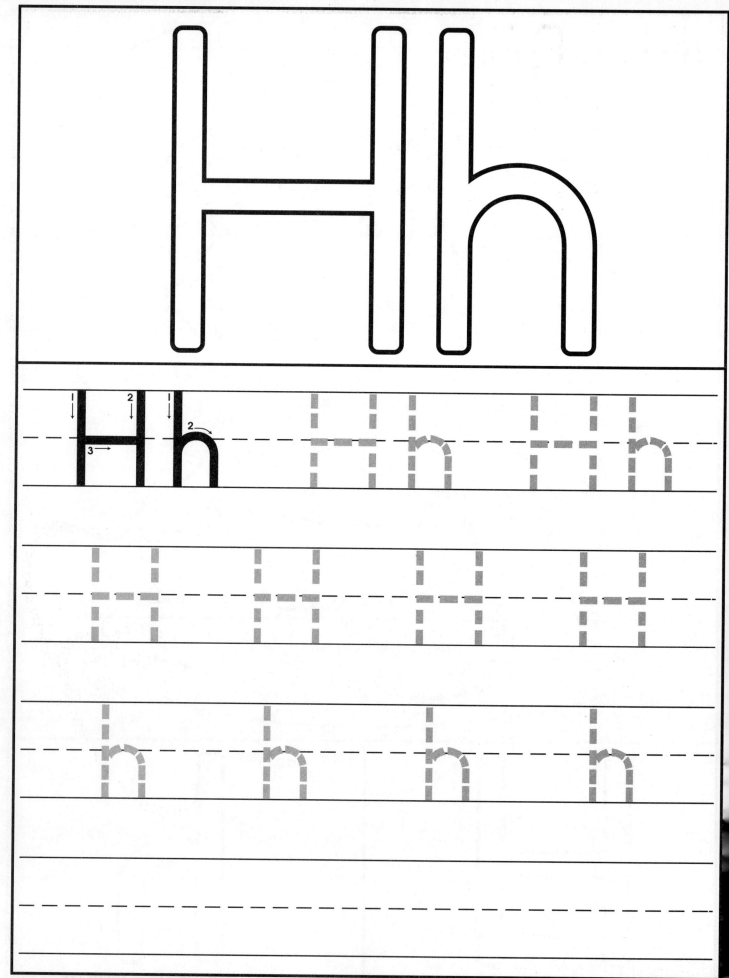

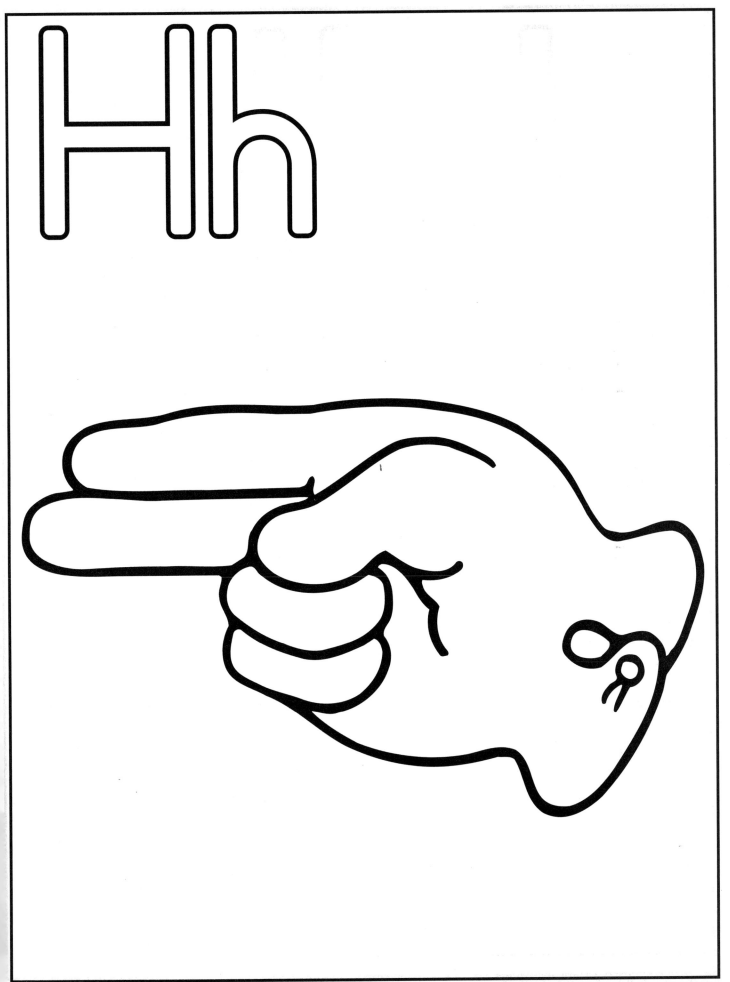

horn	
helicopter	
horse	
hammer	

ice cream

ink

I   i

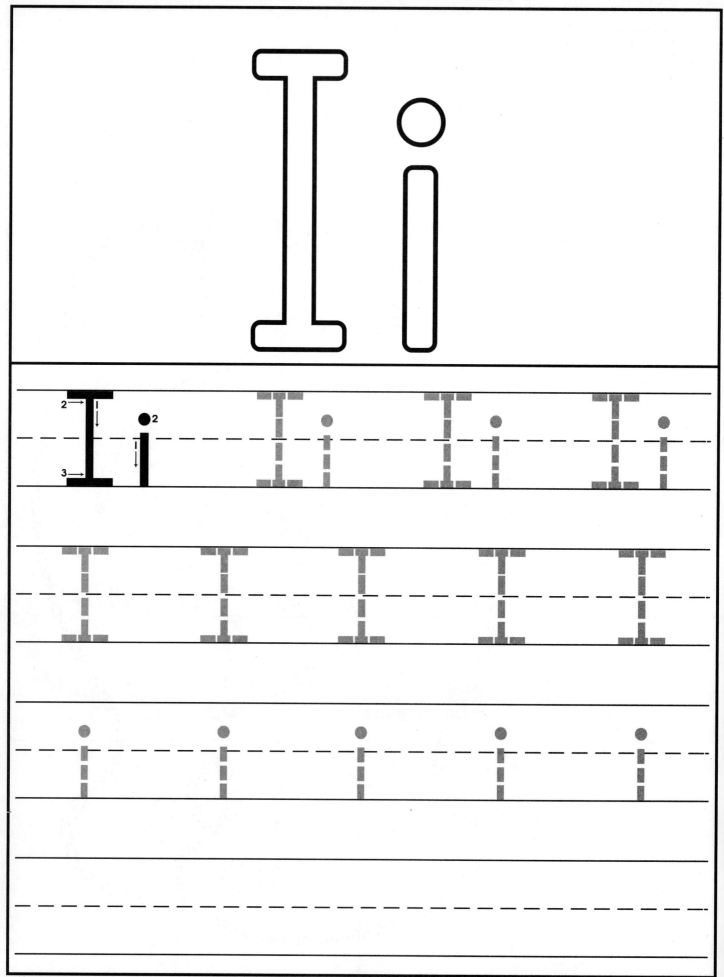

I i

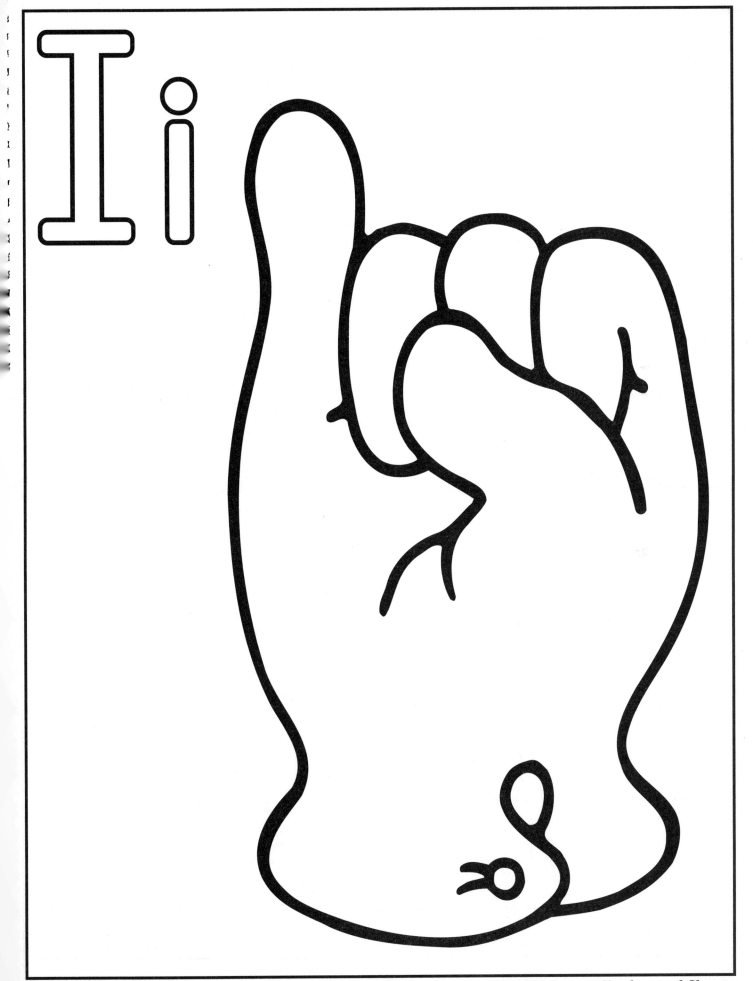

igloo	
Indian	
ice cream	
iron	

juggle
jack-in-the-box

J   j

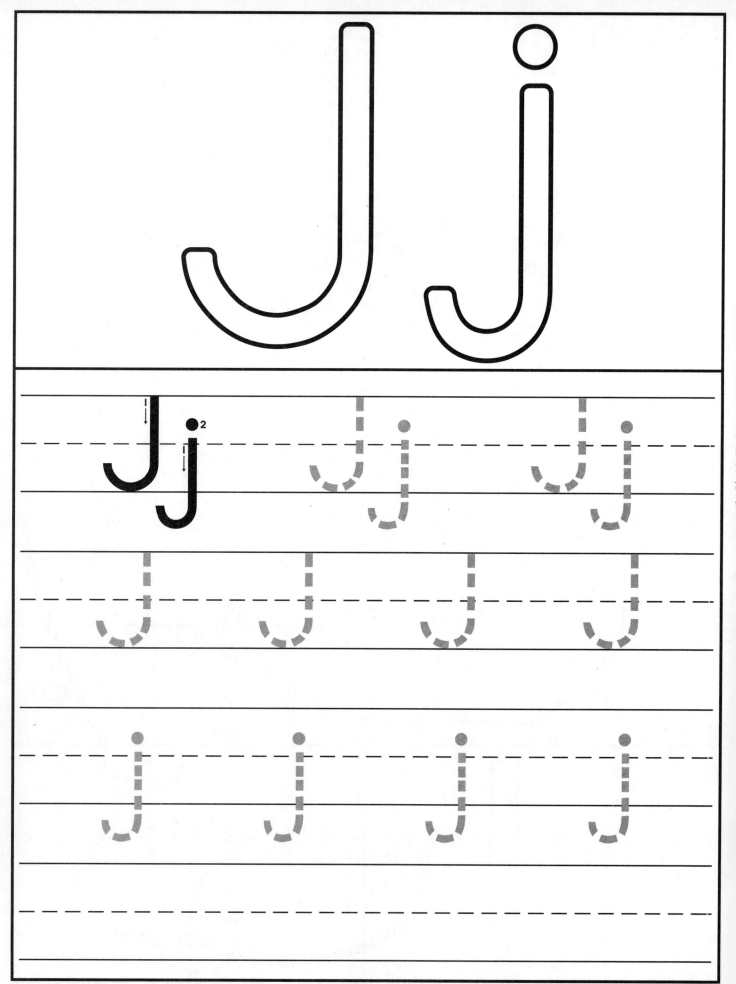

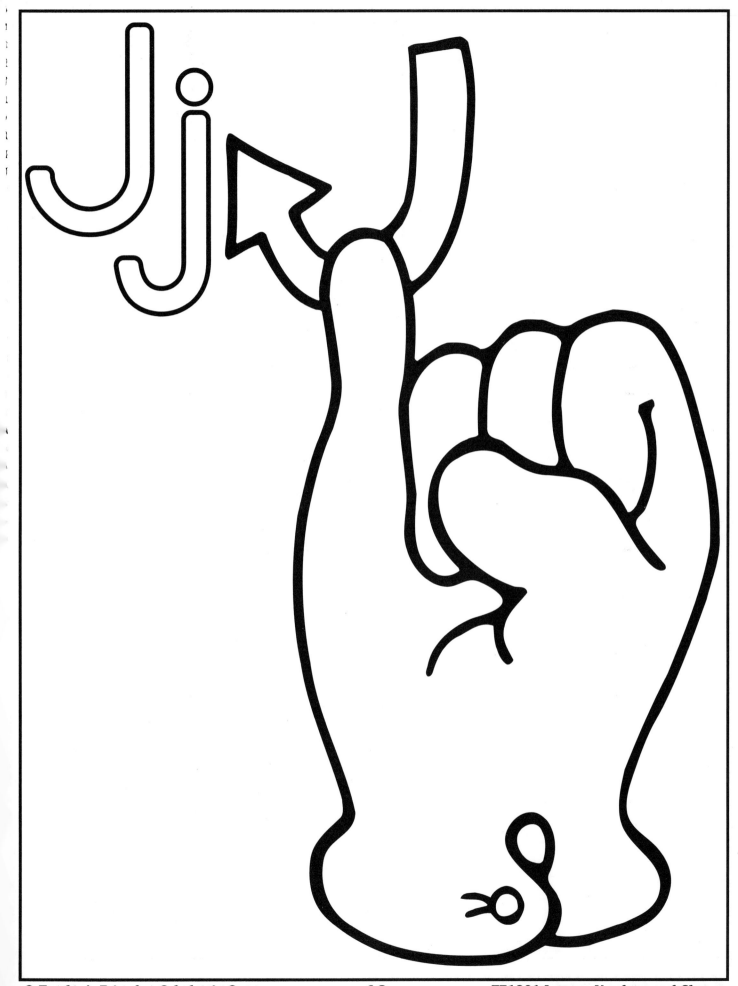

jack-in-the-box	
jack-o'-lantern	
jelly	
jar	

kangaroo
kite

K k

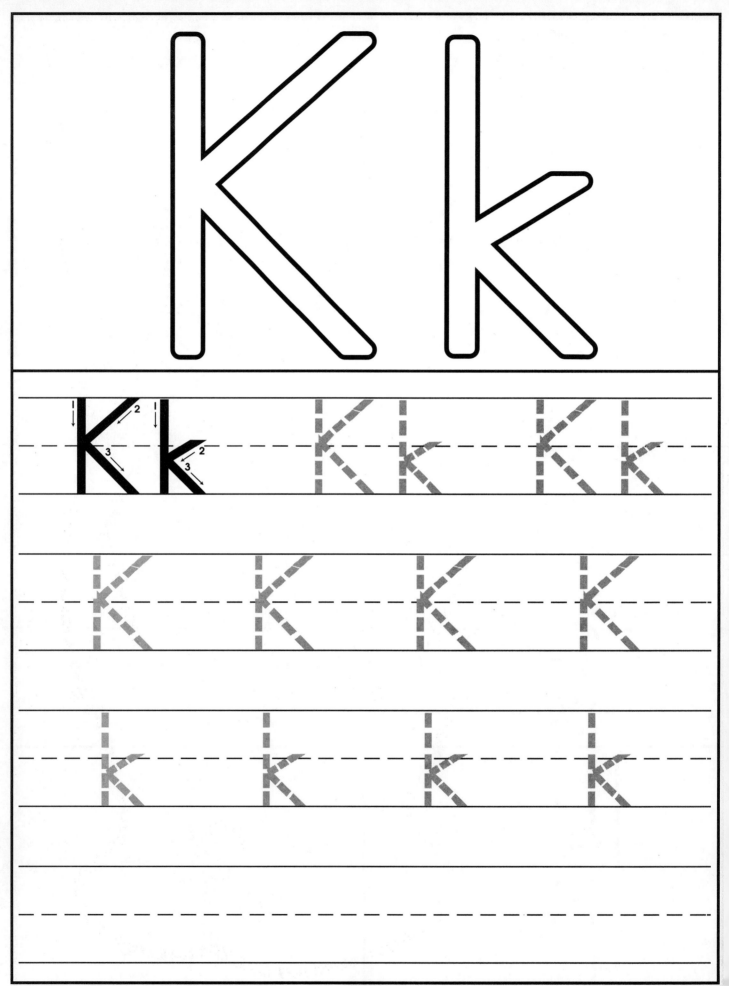

kangaroo	
keys	
king	
kite	

lion
ladder

L

l

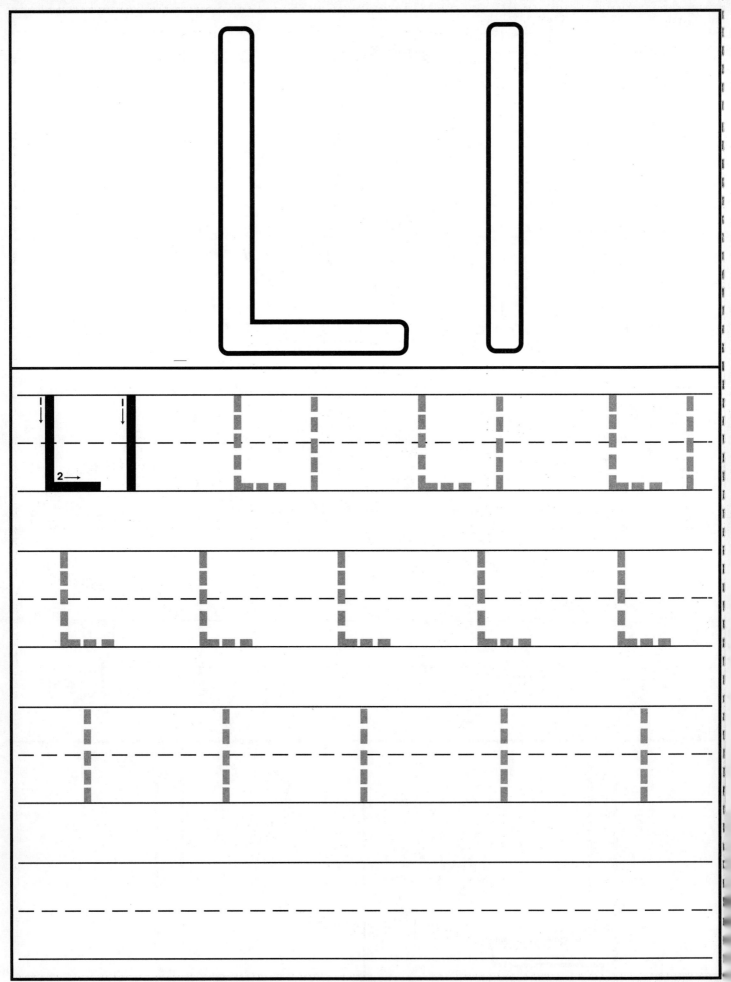

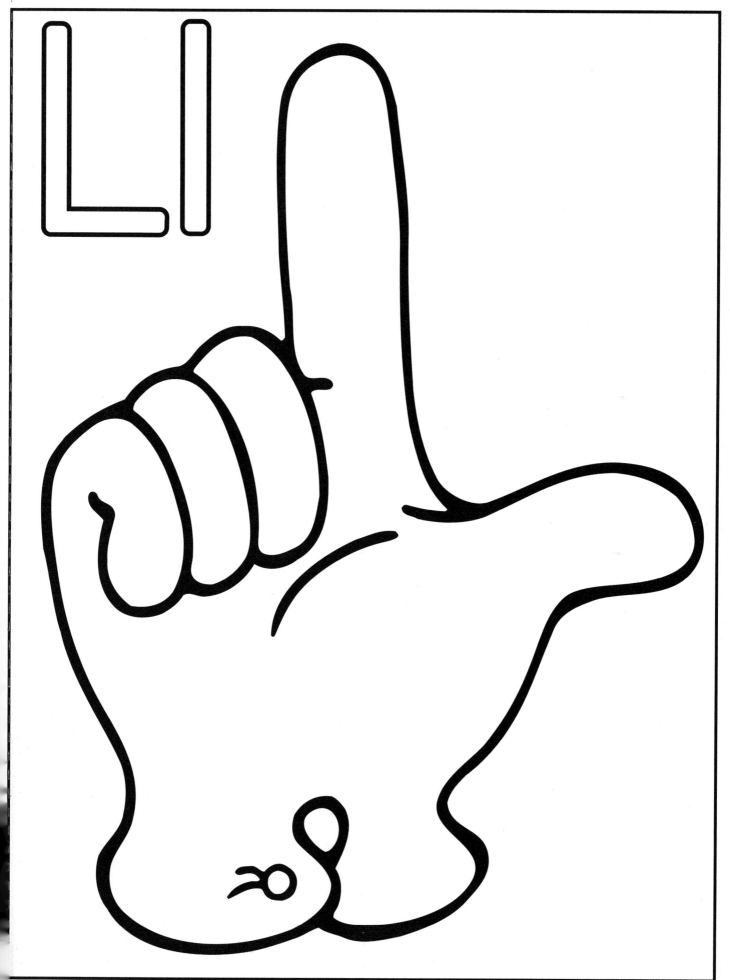

lion

ladder

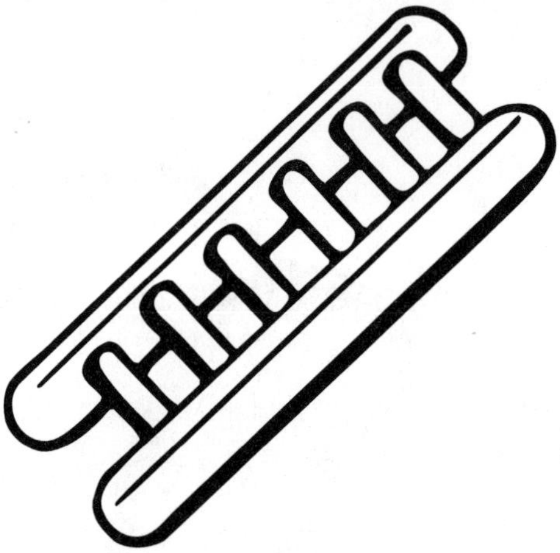

light bulb

lamb

monkey

mirror

M

m

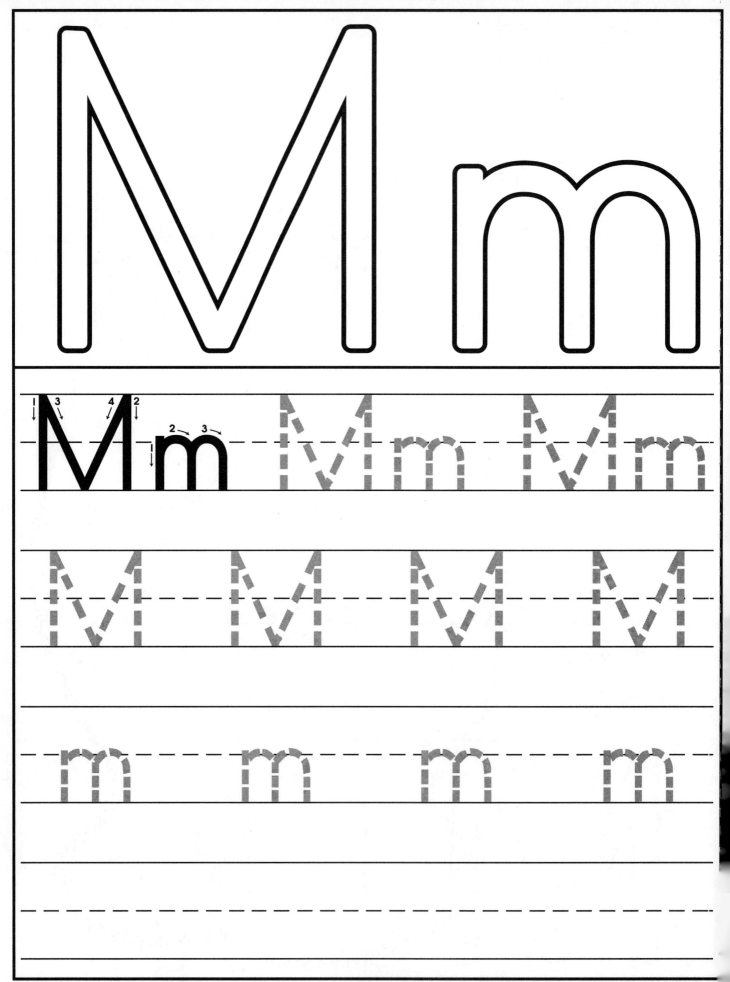

54

Mm

monkey	
mitten	
moon	
mouse	

nose

nest

N

n

Nn

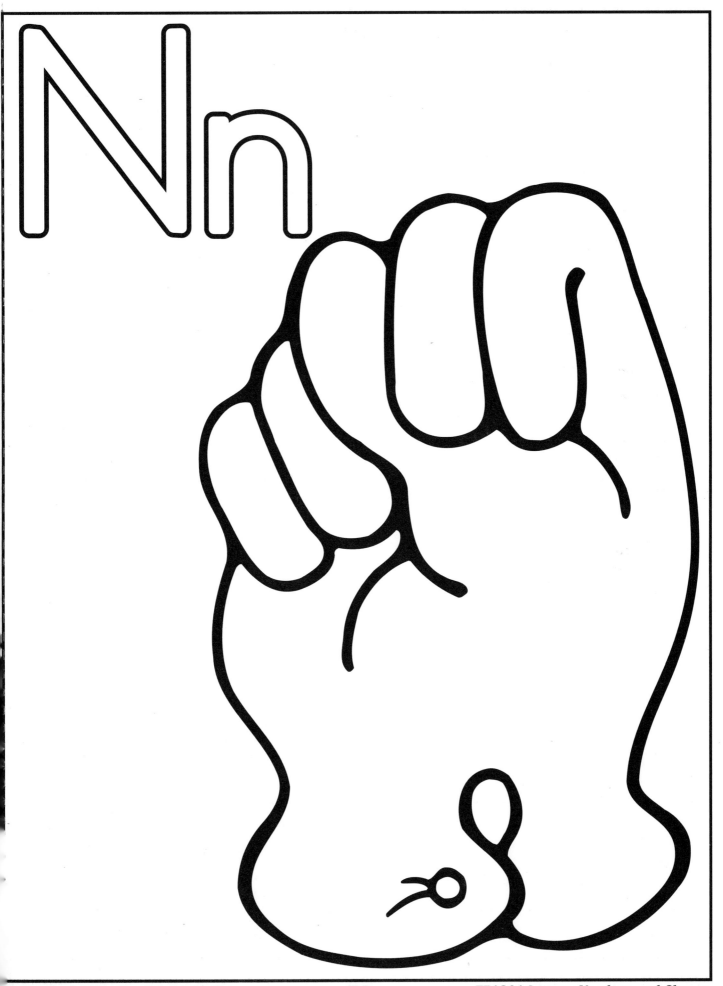

nuts	
needle	
newspaper	
nest	

oranges   octopus

TF1301 Letters, Numbers and Shapes

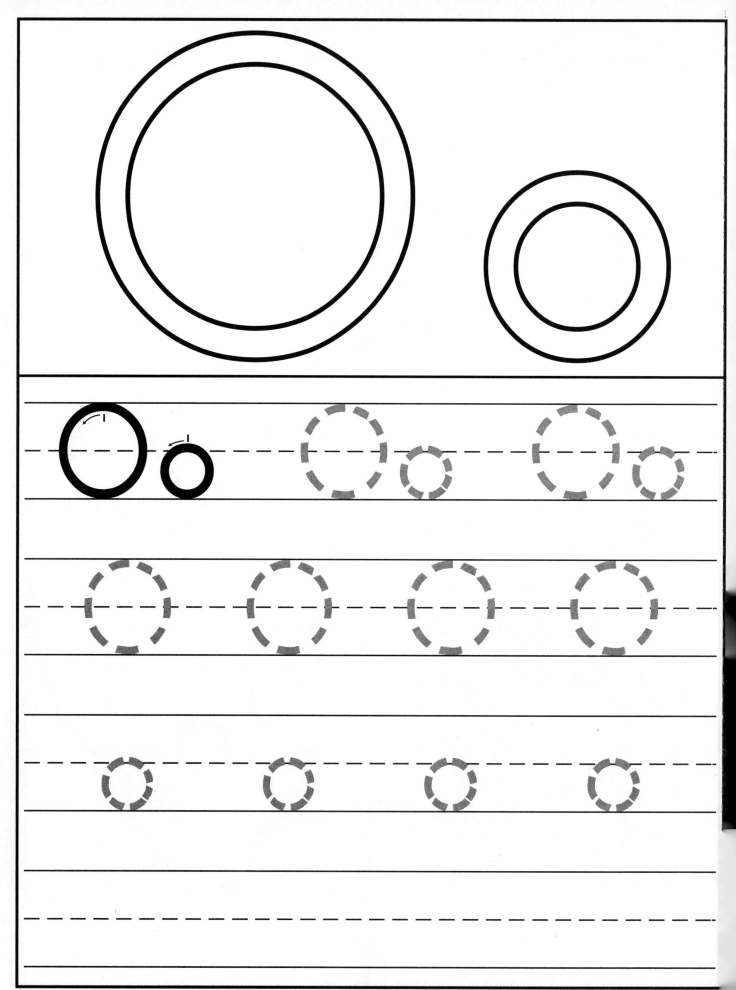

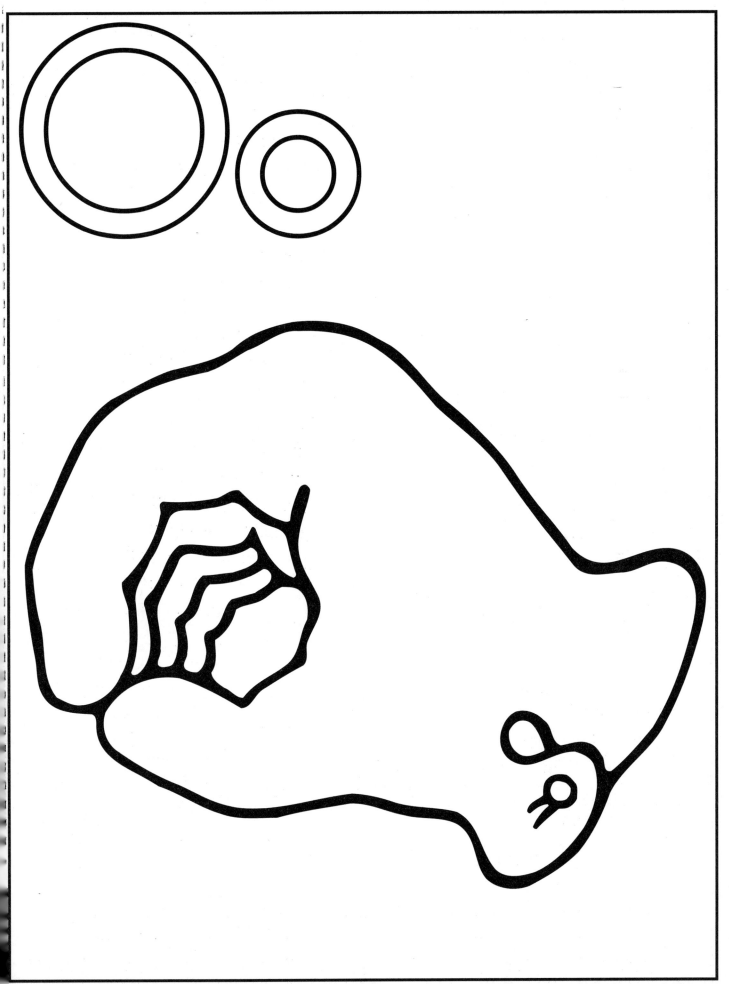

owl	
octopus	
orange	
ostrich	

pig
pencil
paper

P

p

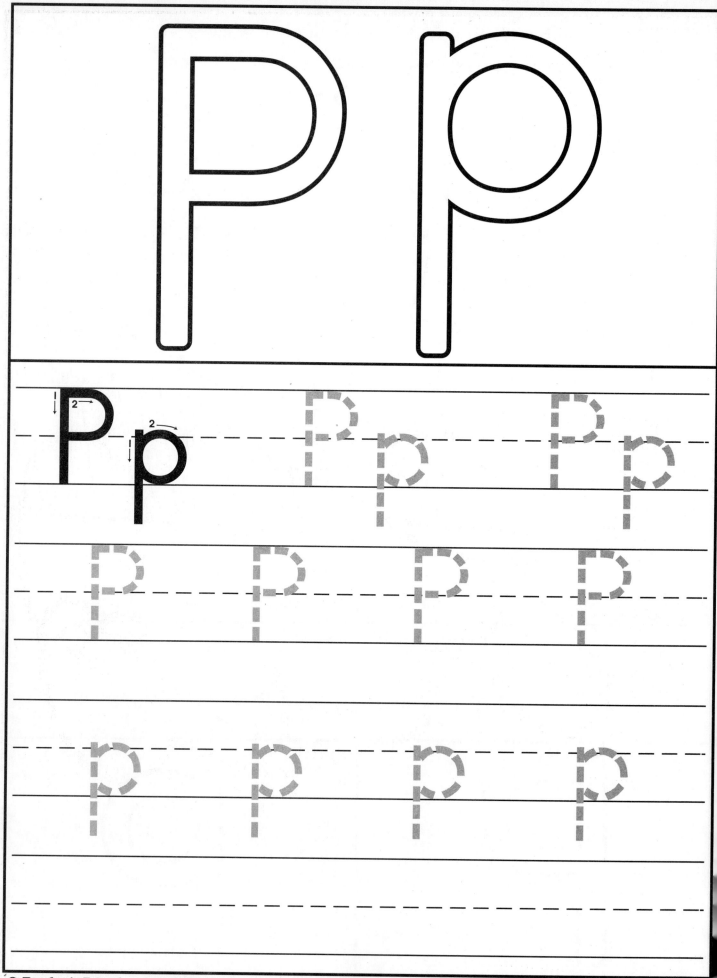

Pp

pencil	
pear	
parachute	
piano	

68

queen
question mark

Q

q

69

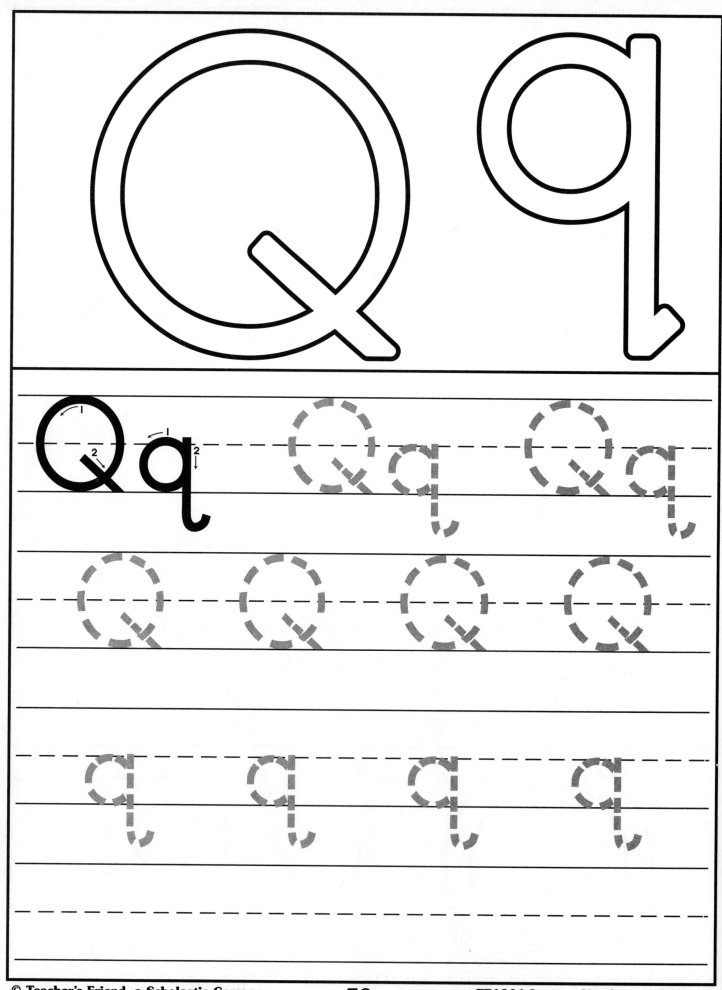

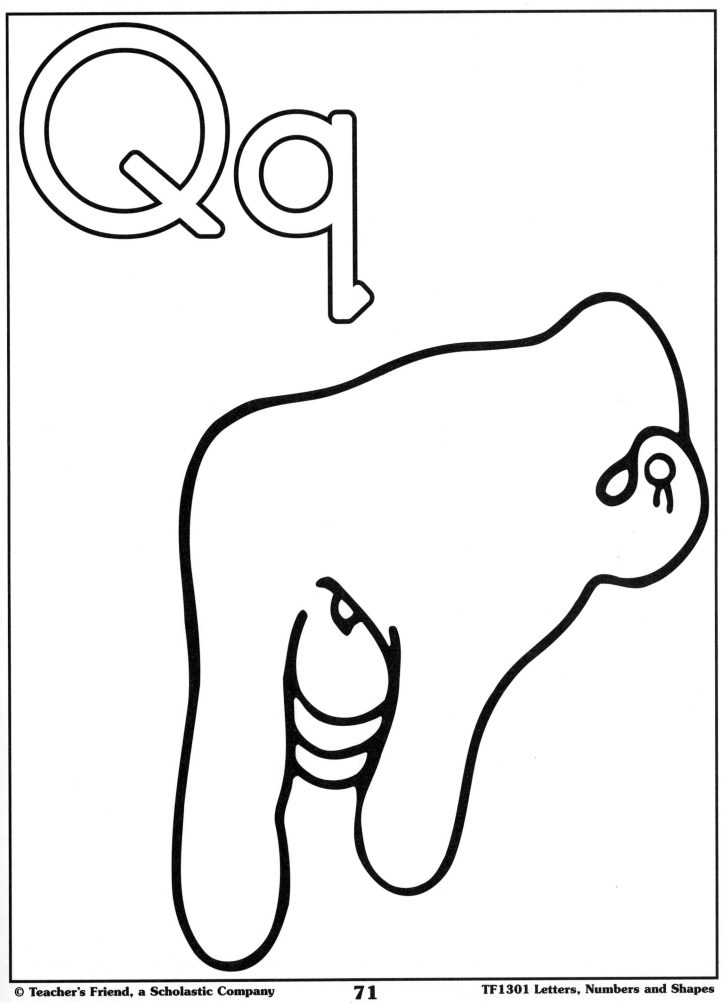

71

quail	
queen	
quilt	
question mark	

rabbit
rocket

R

r

TF1301 Letters, Numbers and Shapes

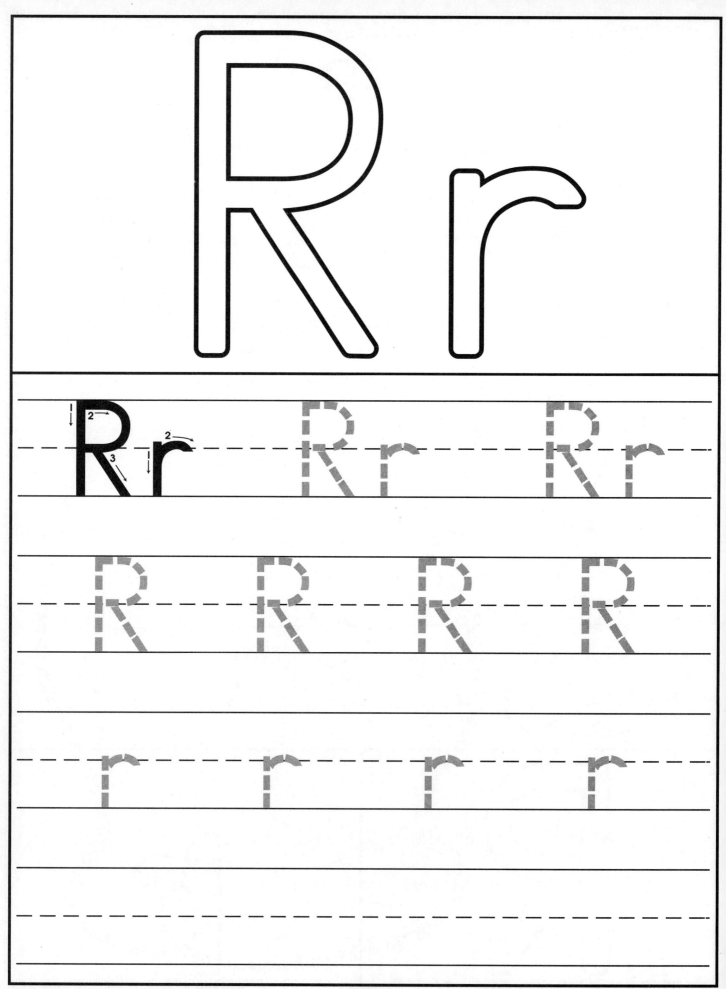

Rr

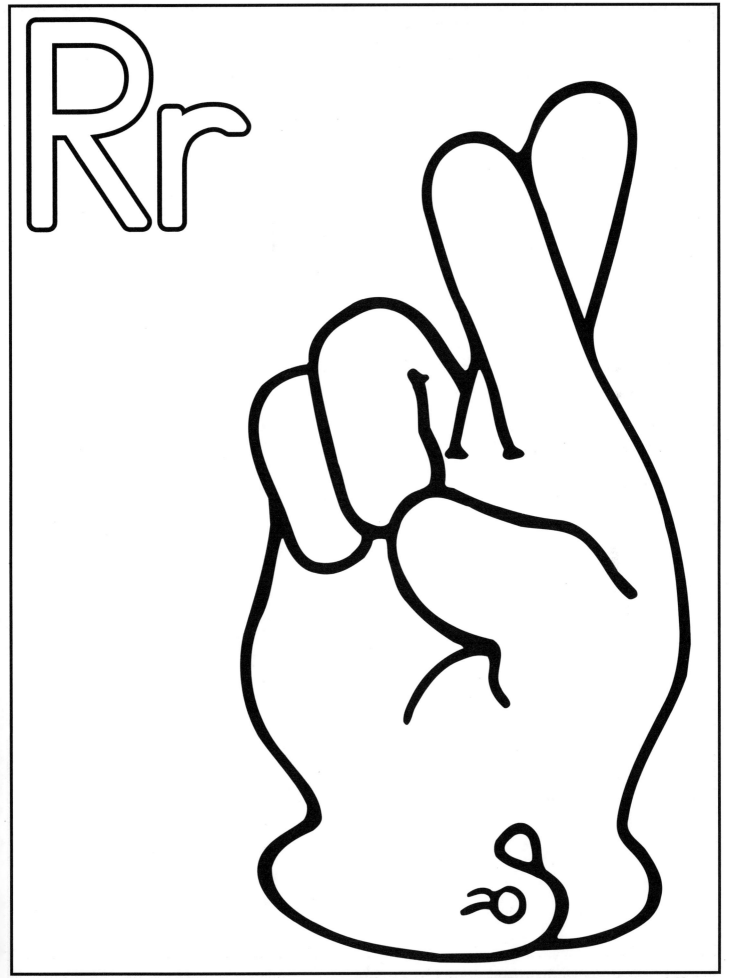

rainbow	
rabbit	
rake	
rocket	

seal
sandwich

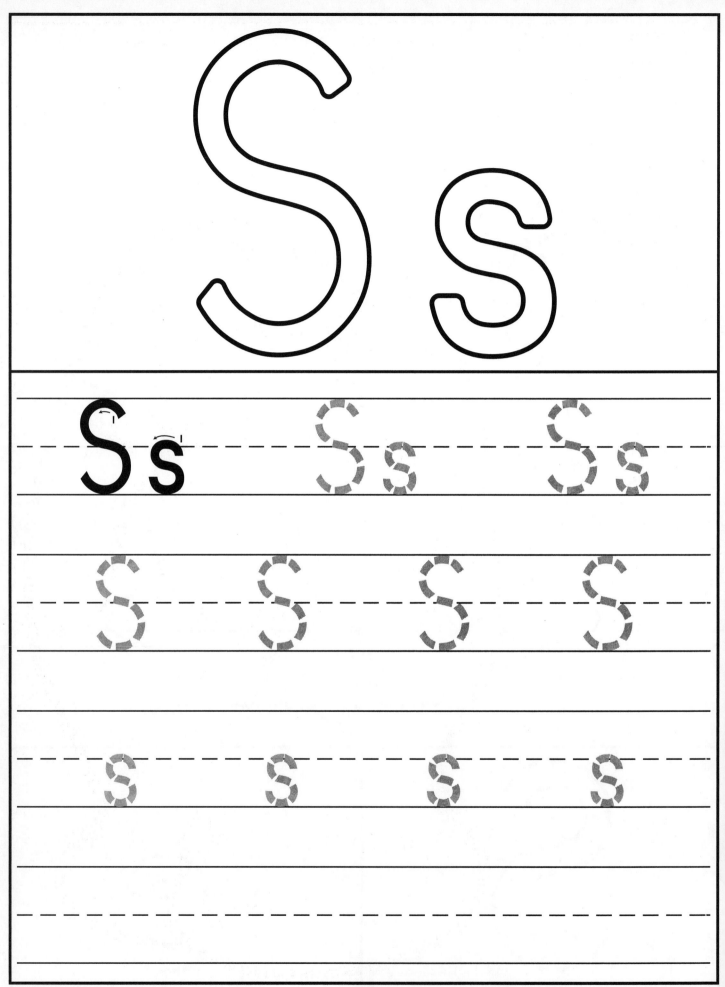

Ss

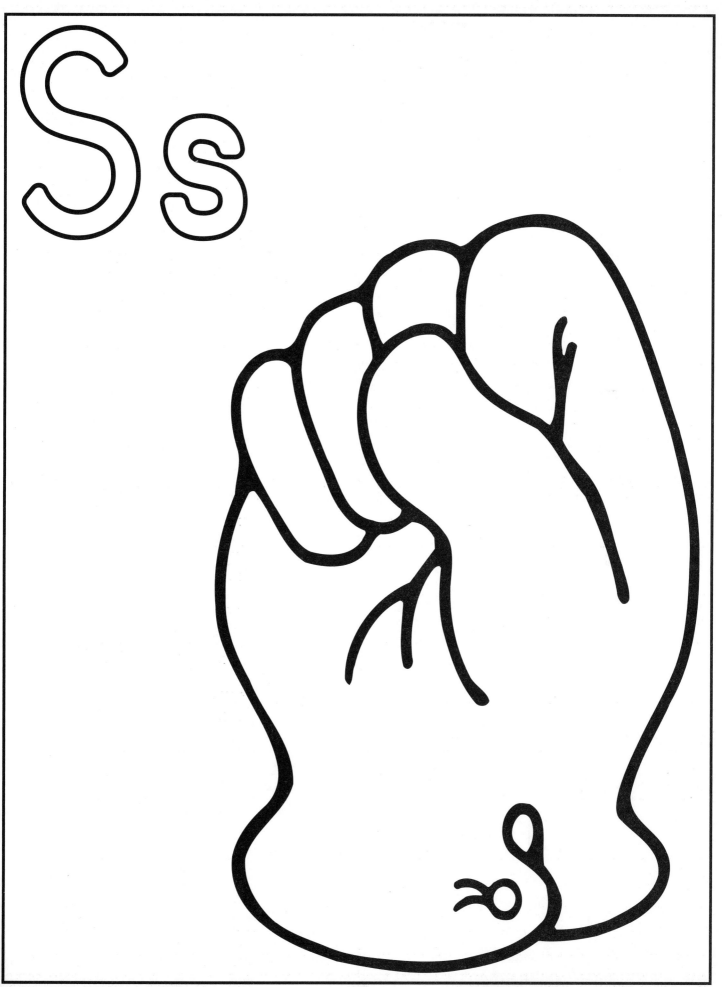

saw	
sun	
soap	
sink	

turtle
top

T   †

TF1301 Letters, Numbers and Shapes

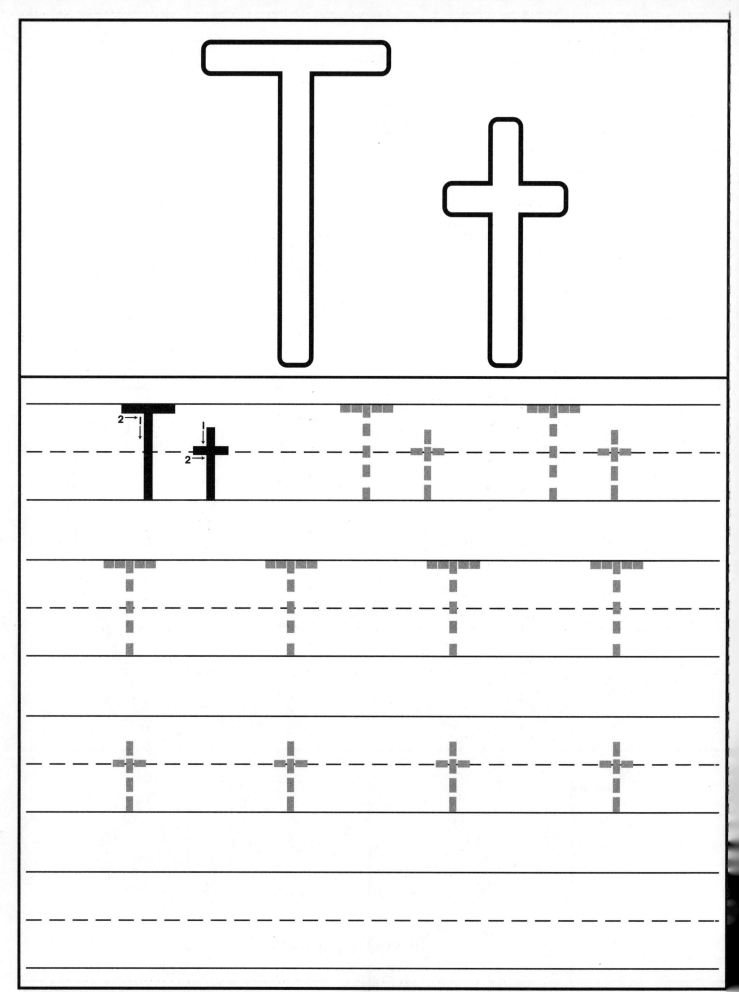

T t

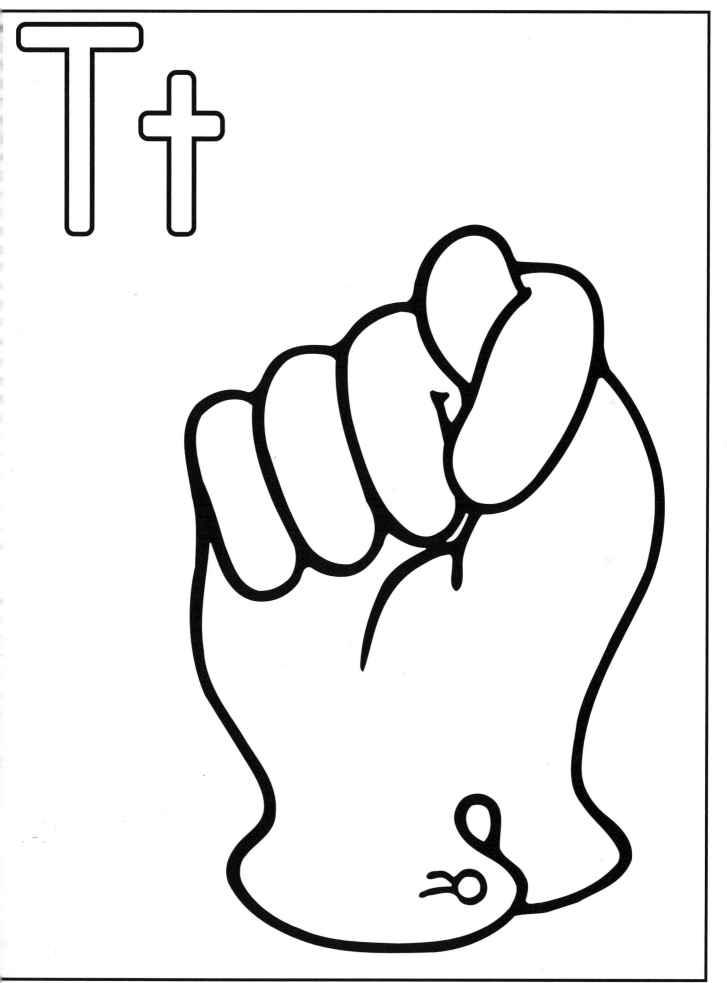

top	
toothbrush	
turtle	
tree	

unicorn
umbrella

U   u

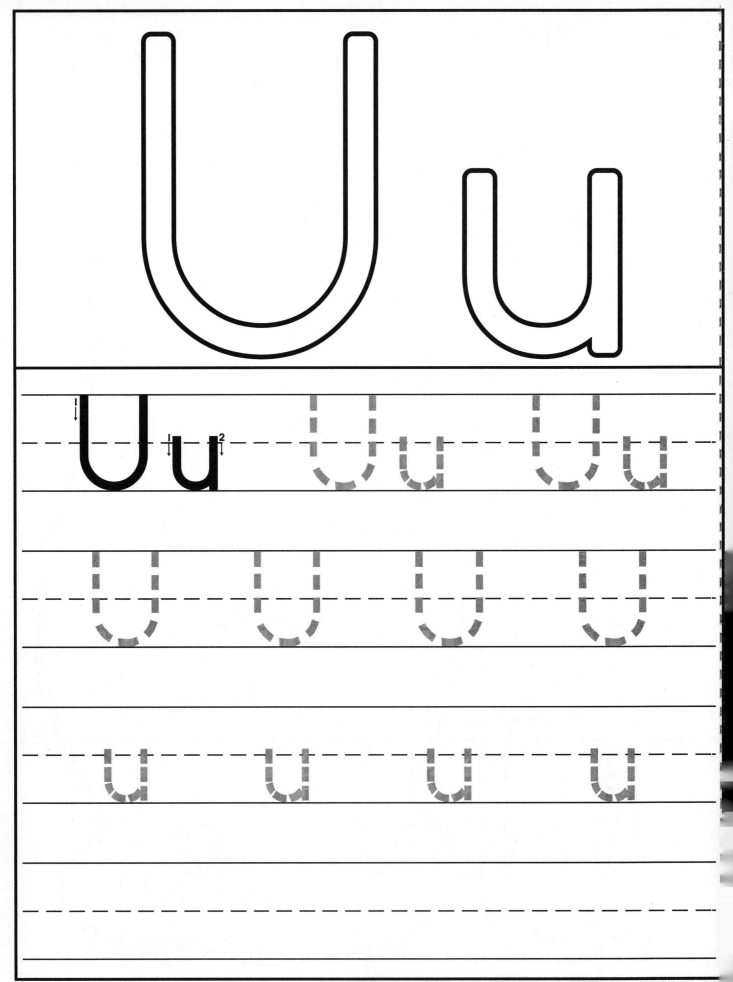

U u

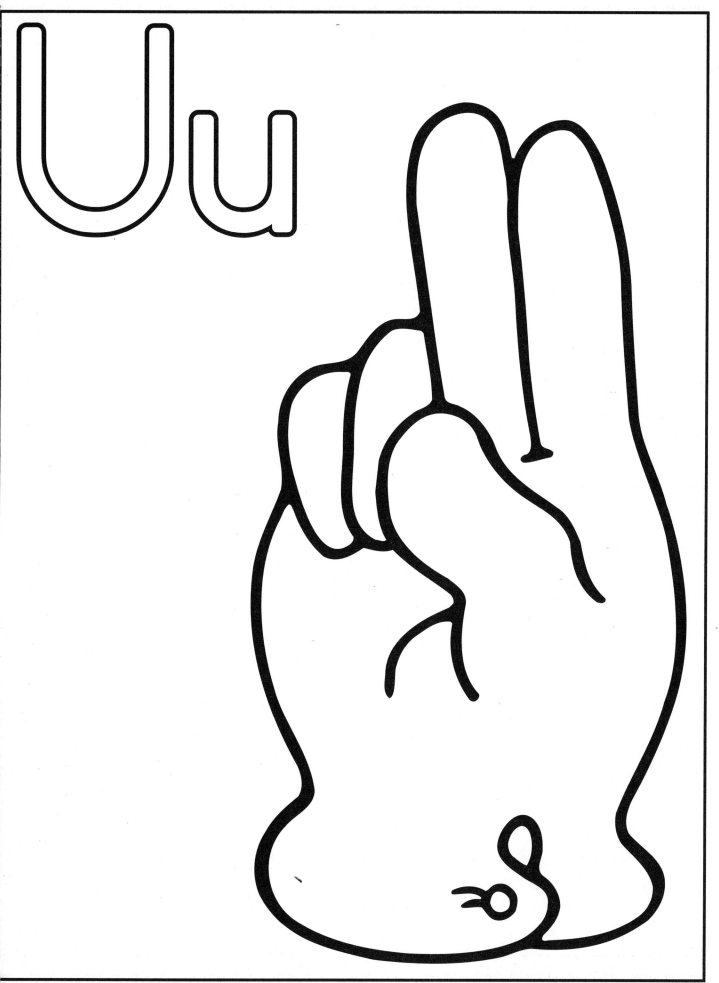

umbrella	
unicorn	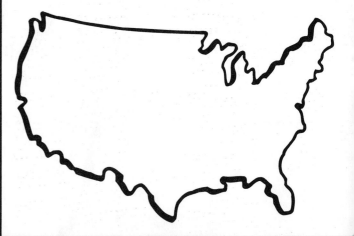
United States	
unicycle	

vampire
valentine

BE
MINE

V   V

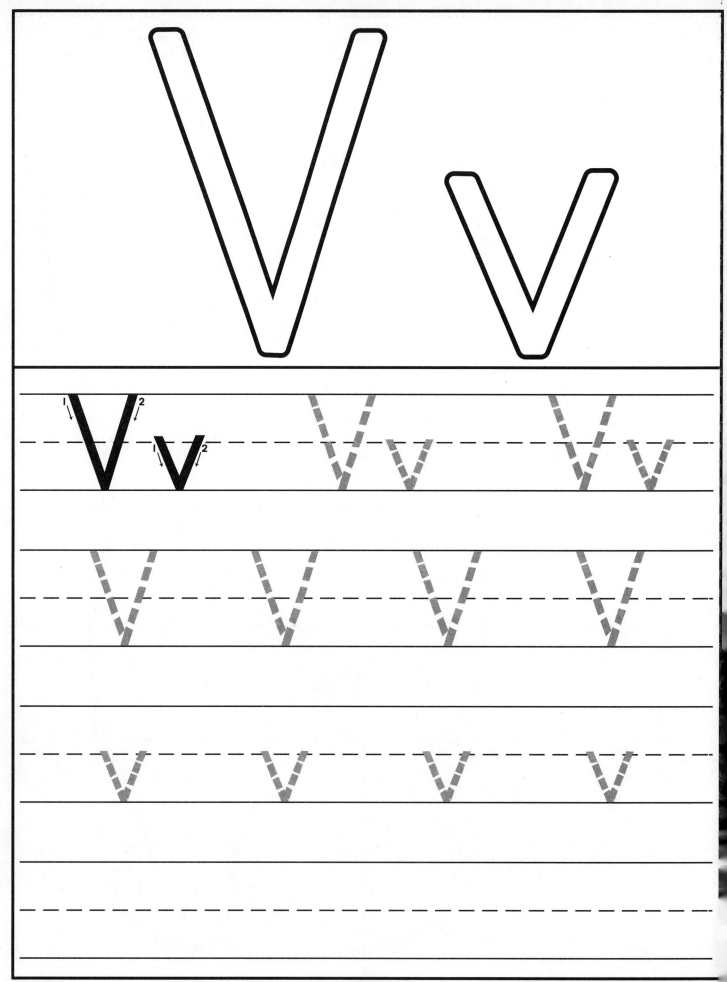

vest	
violin	
valentine	
volcano	

whale
wagon

W

w

TF1301 Letters, Numbers and Shapes

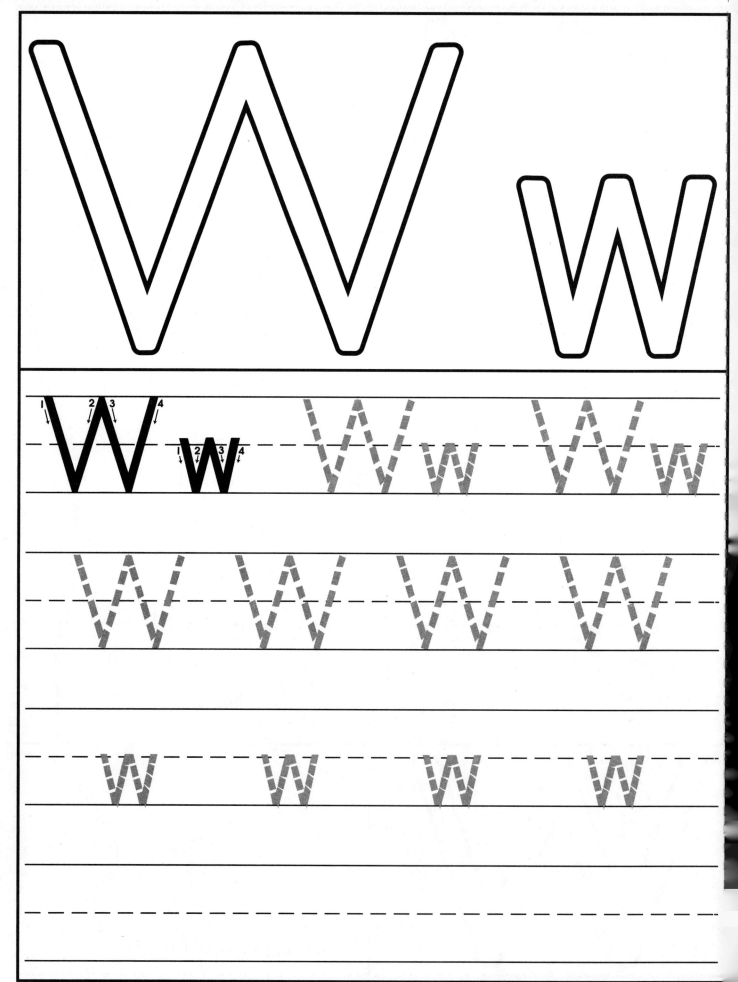

watermelon	
whale	
watch	
wagon	

xylophone
x-ray

X

X

Xx

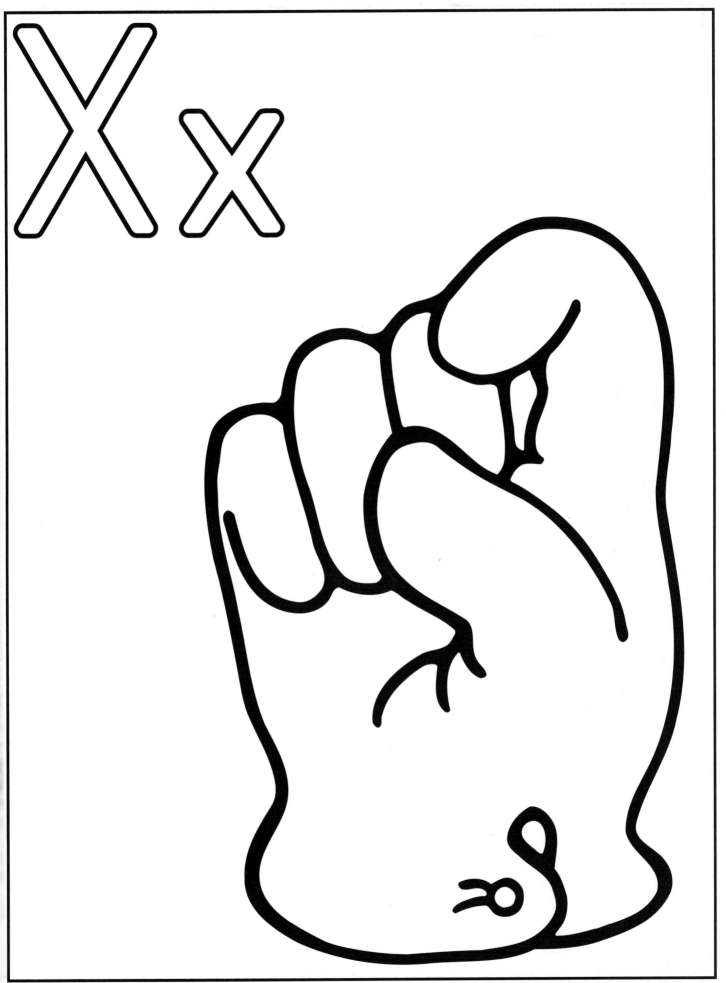

x-ray	
xylophone	

yak

yo-yo

Y

y

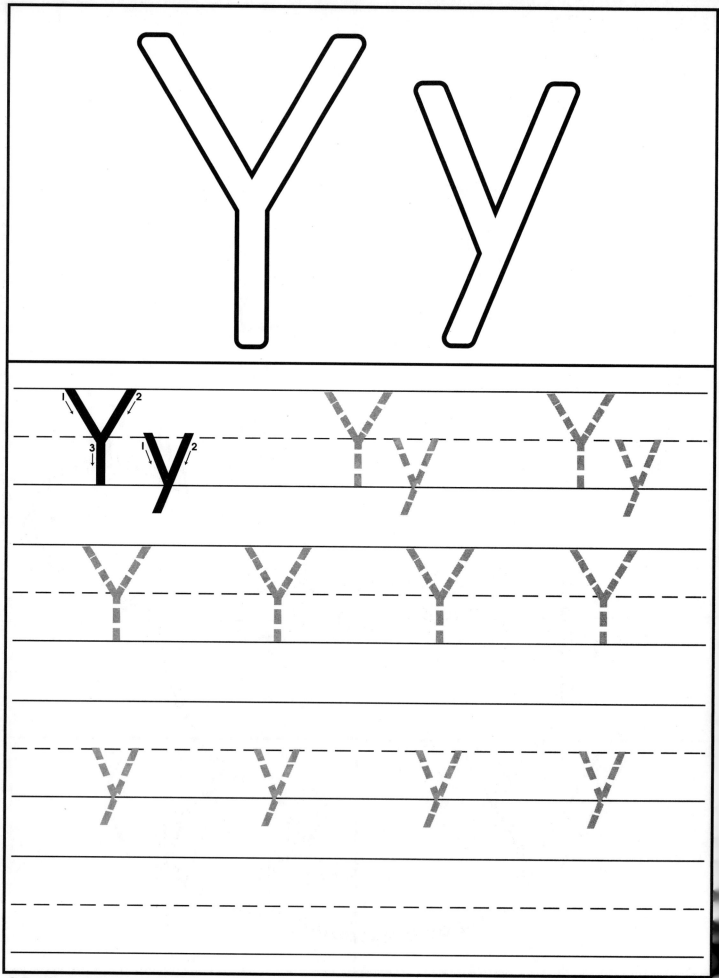

yarn	
yak	
yawn	
yo-yo	

zebra
zipper

Z z

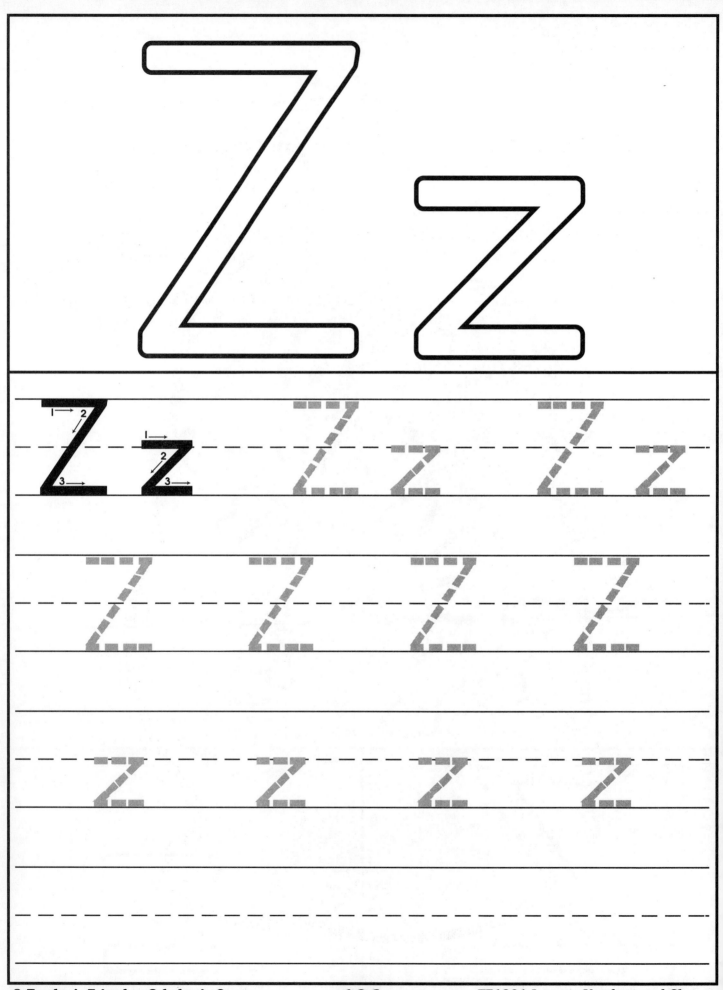

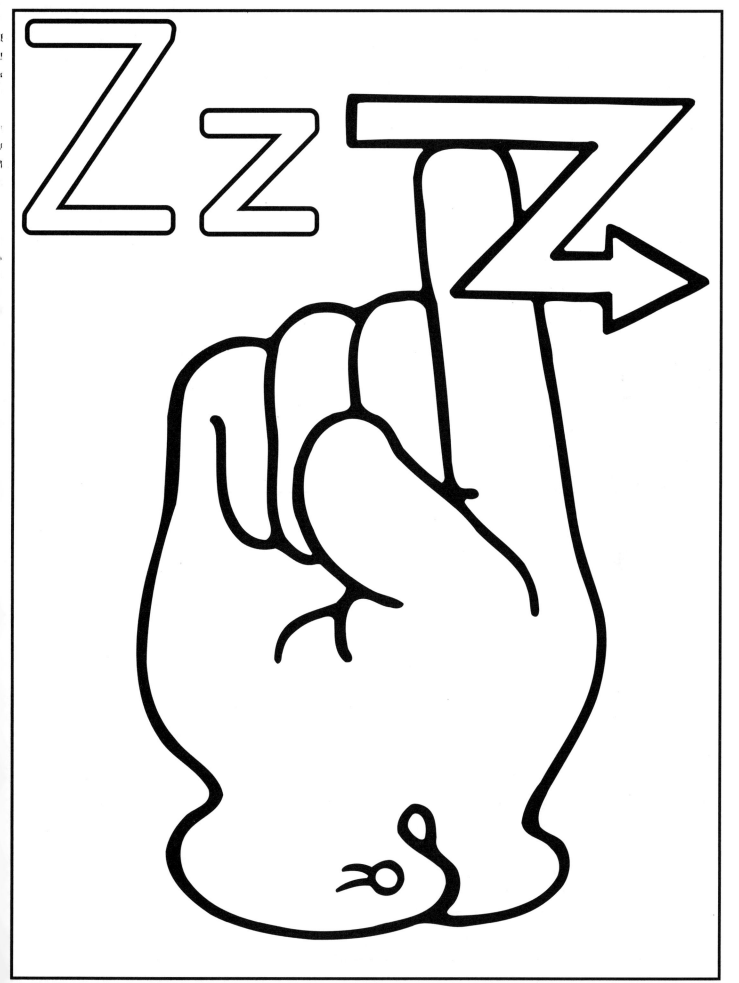

zebra	
zipper	
zero	
zigzag	

Numbers

Numbers 1-30 - Numbers 1-12 are represented by one large numeral and number word card, plus six matching cards. Numbers 13-30 are represented by three matching cards.

Numeral Page - Ask youngsters to color the simple numeral and then paste the appropriate number of items to the numeral. You might want to use one of the following items:

dry cereal	dry pasta
beans	paper clips
stickers	buttons
pennies	cotton balls
marshmallows	fish crackers
candies	rubber bands

Cut the number word card from the bottom of the page and ask students to match the number word to the numeral.

Matching Numbers - Matching numeral, number word and counting cards helps your children practice simple math concepts and recognize math words. (Ordinal numbers and Roman numerals are also included for numbers 1-12.)

Cut the cards apart and mount them on squares of poster board. Laminate the cards for durability.

Young learners will learn to sort, group and count while matching the cards. They will also begin to recognize specific number words. As additional numbers are introduced and mastered, more cards can be added to the matching activity.

Student-Made Number Posters - Young children can make a simple poster for each number 1-12. Have the children color and cut out the pages for each specific number. The elements can be arranged and pasted to a large sheet of construction paper. As each number is introduced and mastered, have your students make the posters and take them home to share with parents.

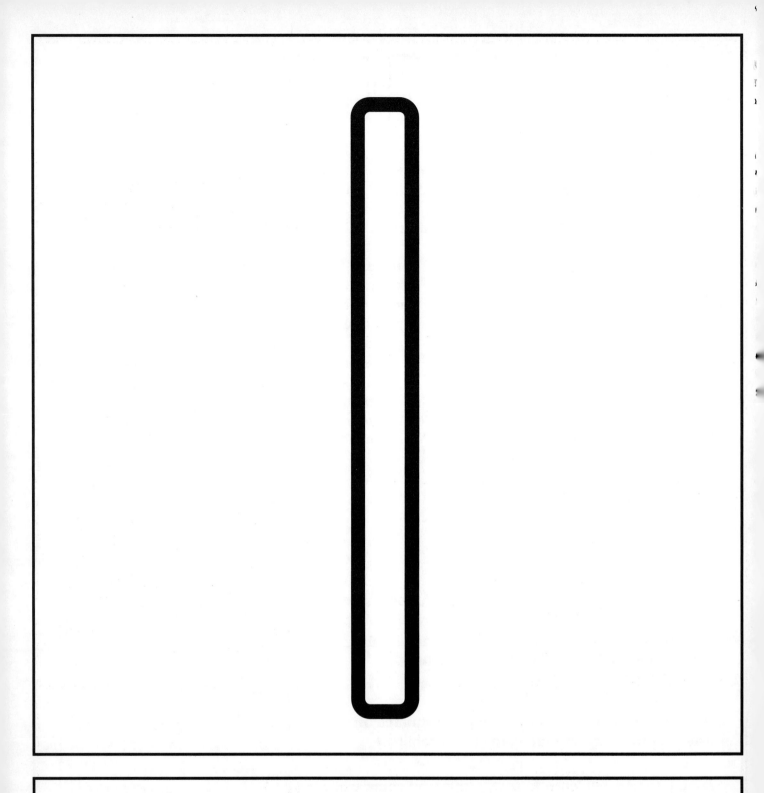

I	one
O	
I	first

TF1301 Letters, Numbers and Shapes

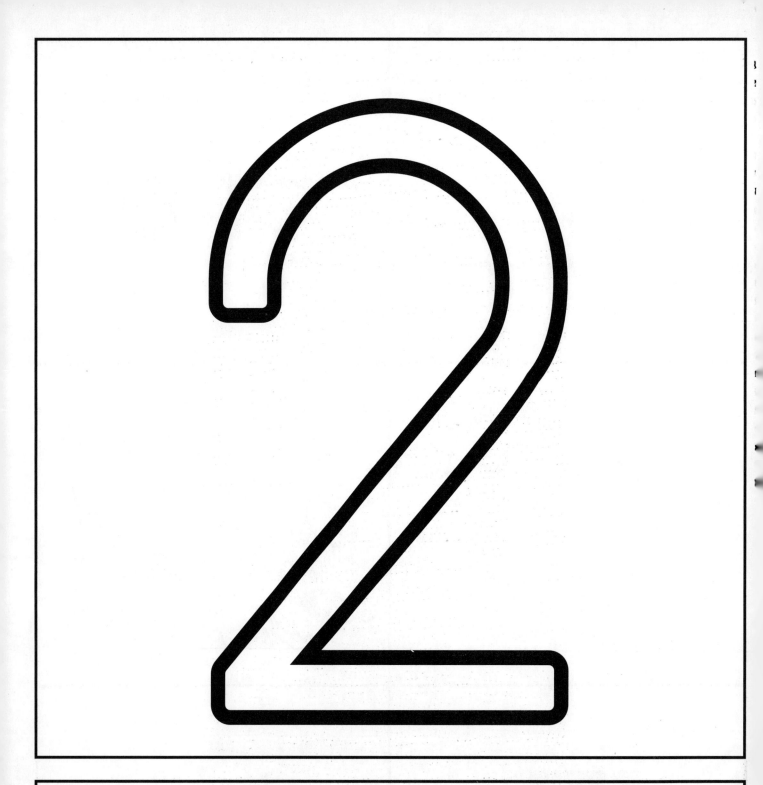

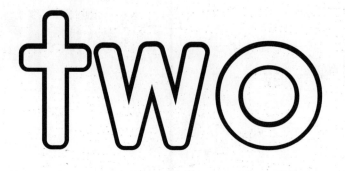

2

†two

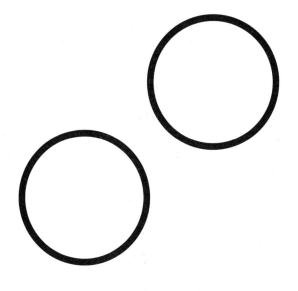

Ⅱ

second

113 TF1301 Letters, Numbers and Shapes

3

three

III

third

4

four

IV

fourth

5

five

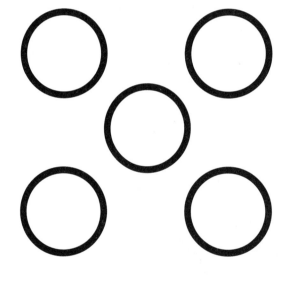

ⴲ

fifth

TF1301 Letters, Numbers and Shapes

6

six

Ⅵ

sixth

7

seven

VII

seventh

8

eight

VIII

eighth

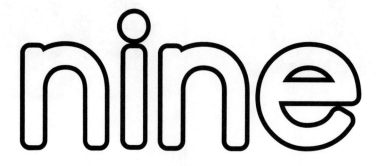

9

nine

IX

ninth

TF1301 Letters, Numbers and Shapes

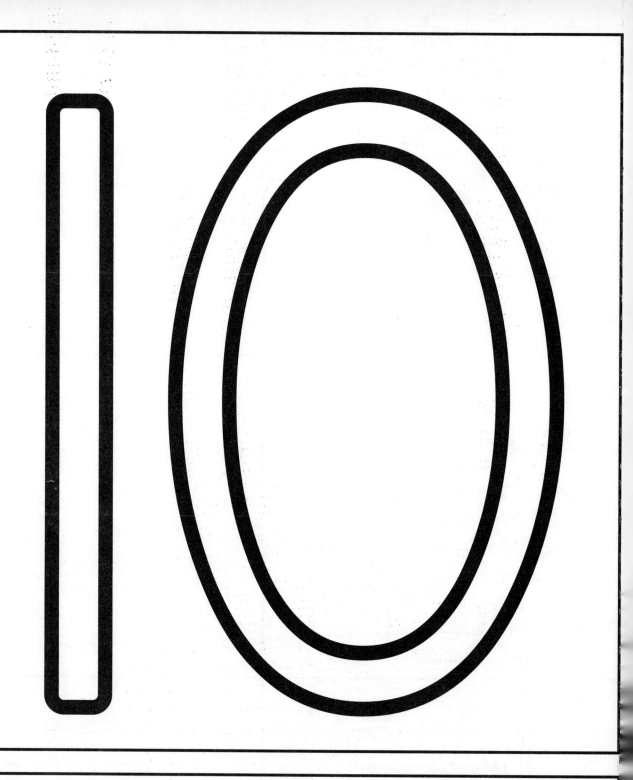

10	ten
⊗⊗⊗⊗⊗ (ten circles)	(ten bugs)
Ⅹ	tenth

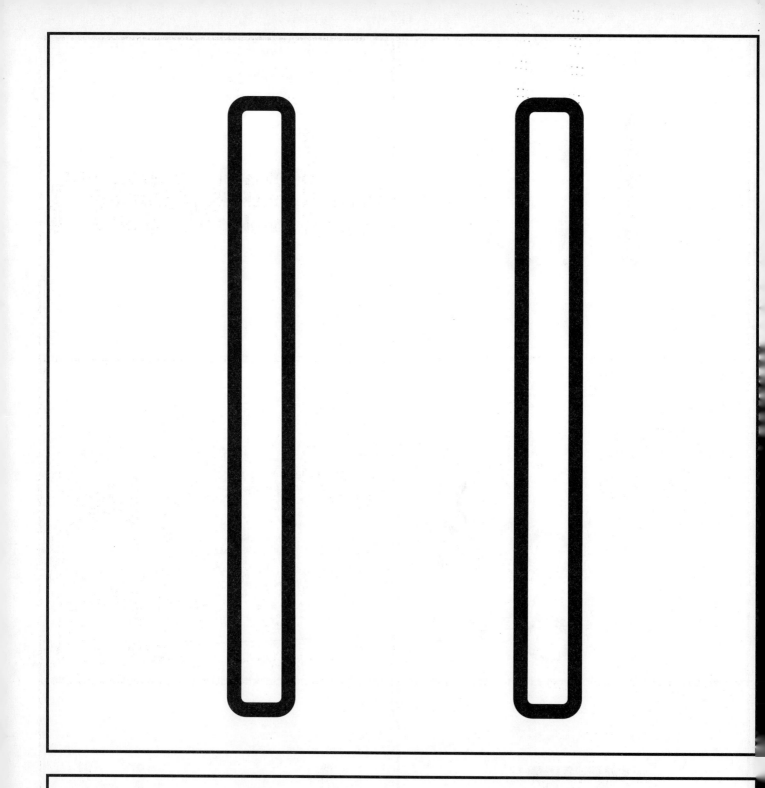

11

eleven

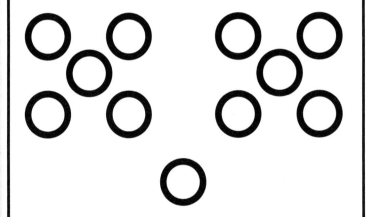

XI

eleventh

TF1301 Letters, Numbers and Shapes

twelve

132 TF1301 Letters, Numbers and Shapes

12

twelve

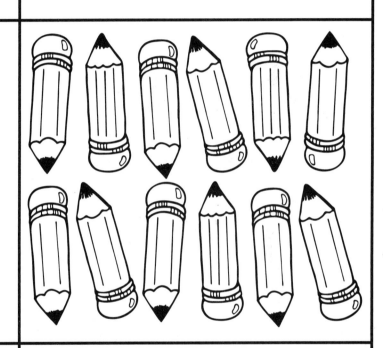

XII

twelfth

13

thirteen

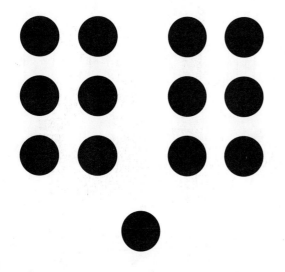

14

fourteen

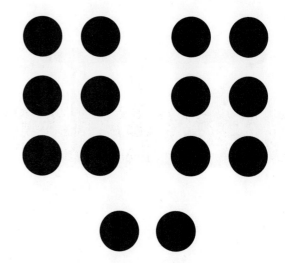

15

fifteen

16

sixteen

17

seventeen

18

eighteen

19

nineteen

20

twenty

21

twenty-one

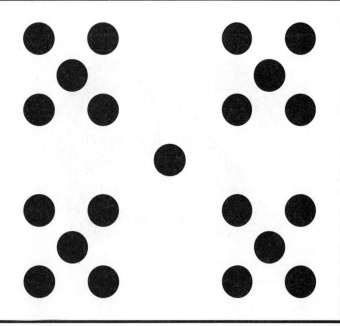

22

twenty-two

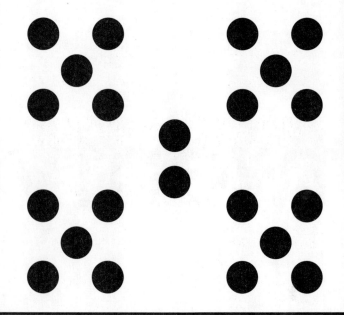

23

twenty-three

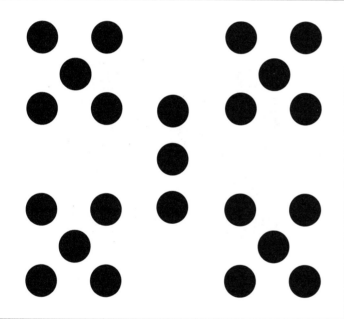

24

twenty-four

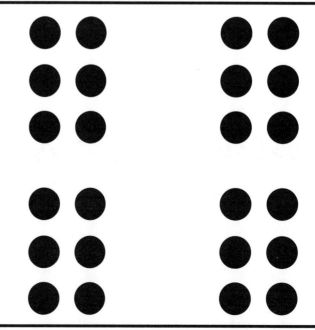

25

twenty-five

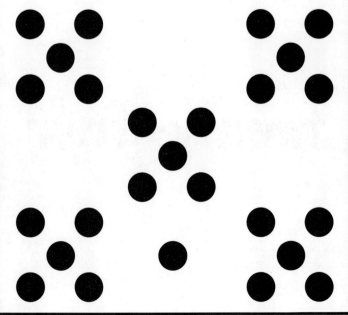

26

twenty-six

27

twenty-seven

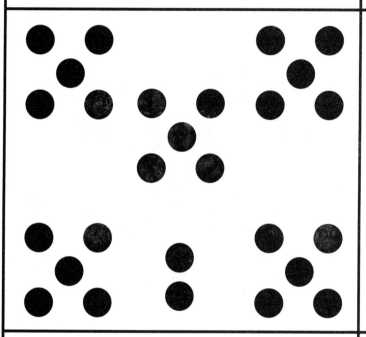

28

twenty-eight

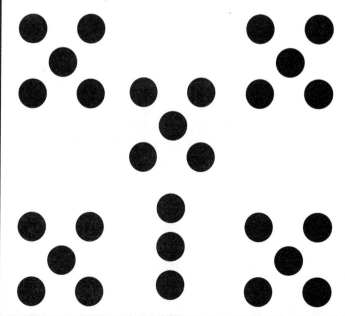

29

twenty-nine

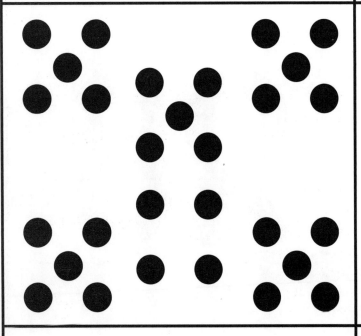

30

thirty

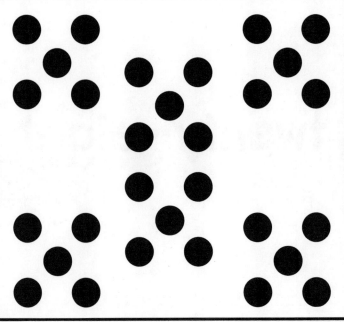

TF1301 Letters, Numbers and Shapes

Shapes

Nine different shapes are represented on these reproducible pages. They include these geometric shapes: circle, square, triangle, rectangle, star, diamond, oval, hexagon and pentagon.

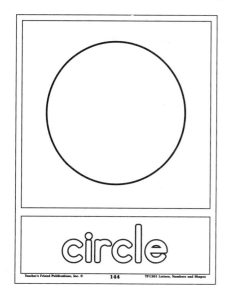

Shape Page - Ask youngsters to color the simple geometric shape and then paste appropriate shaped items to the shape. Cut the various shapes from colored paper for the youngsters to paste in place. Items such as dried cereal and pasta in the shapes of circles and squares can also be used.

Matching Shapes - Matching shapes and shape words helps young children practice simple geometric concepts and recognize math words.

Cut the cards apart and mount them on squares of poster board. Laminate the cards for durability.

Young learners will learn to identify, sort, group, and match the cards. They will also begin to recognize specific shape words. As additional shapes are introduced and mastered, more cards can be added to the matching activity.

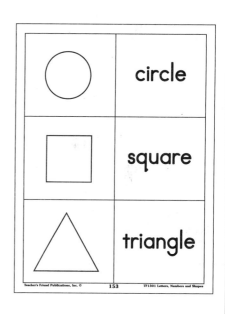

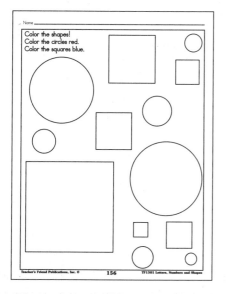

Color the Shapes - Have youngsters practice their knowledge of simple shapes. Ask students to identify the simple shapes and color them the appropriate colors.

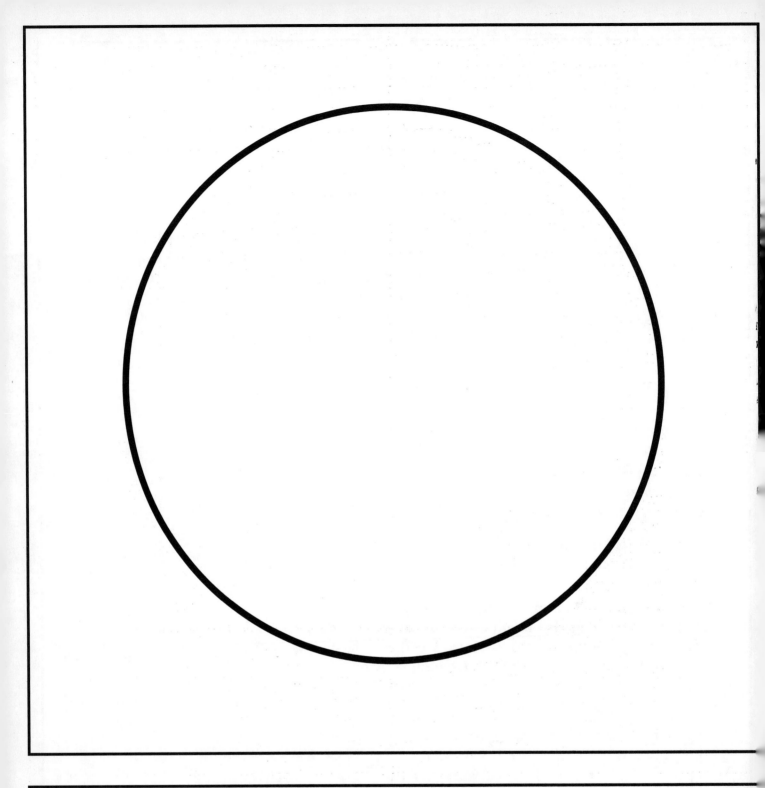

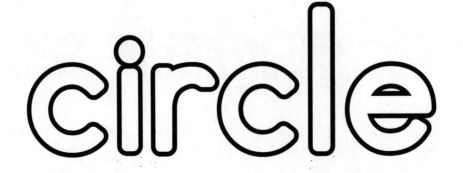

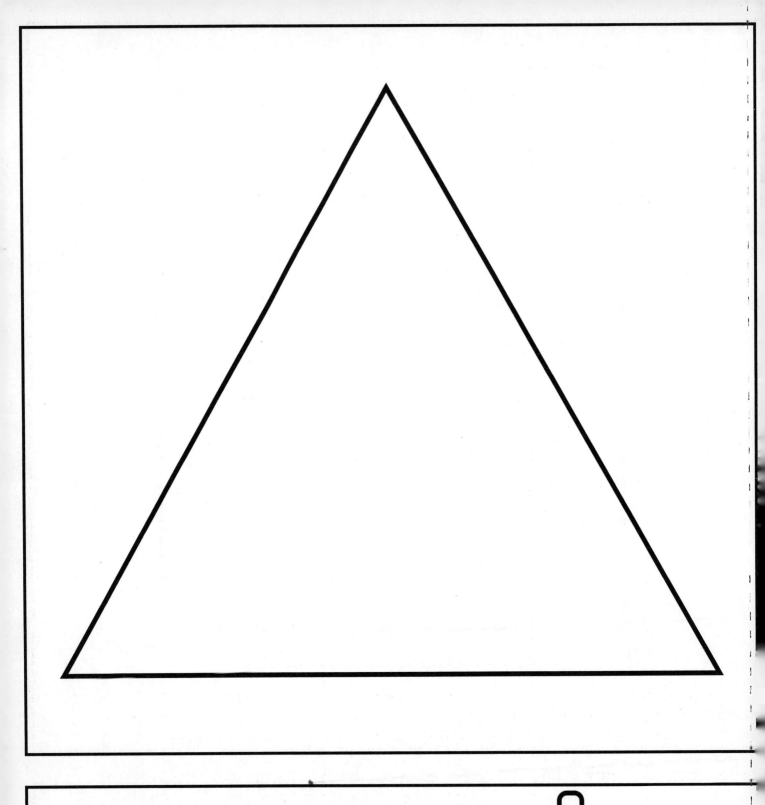

triangle

146

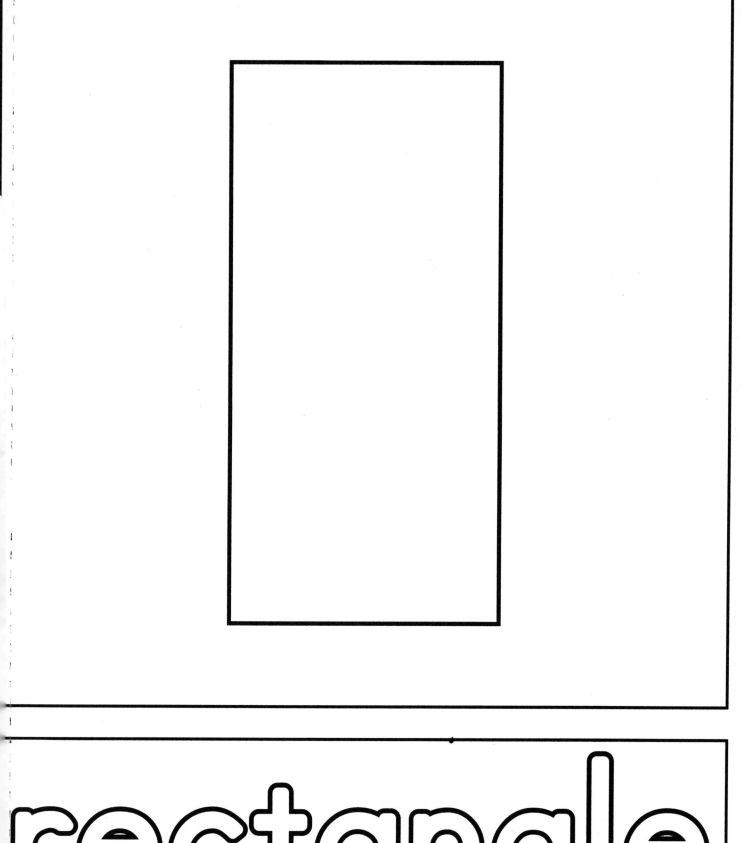

rectangle

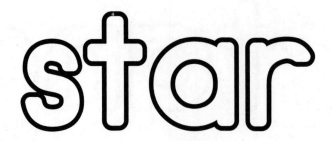

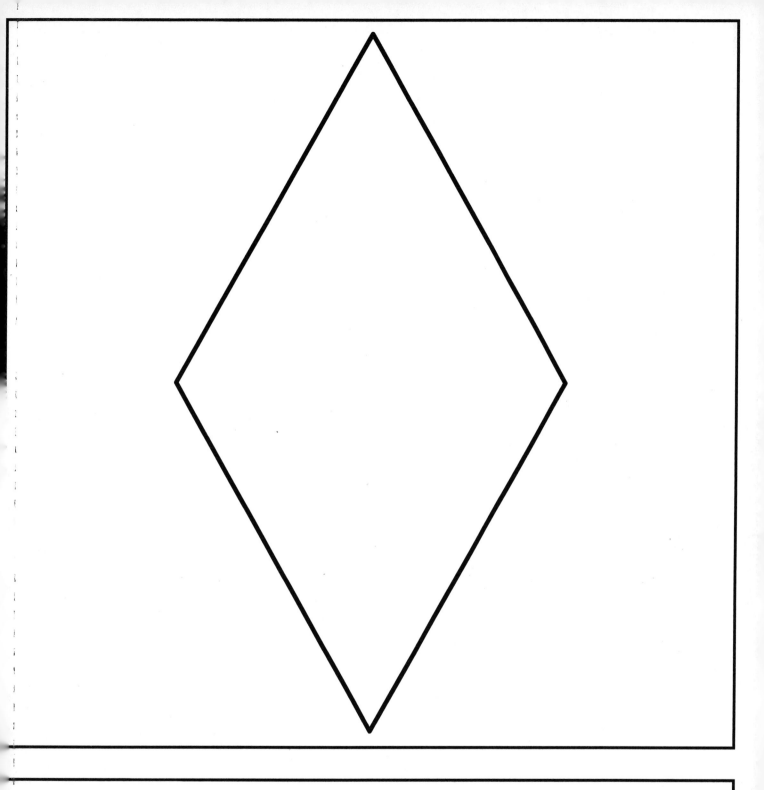

diamond

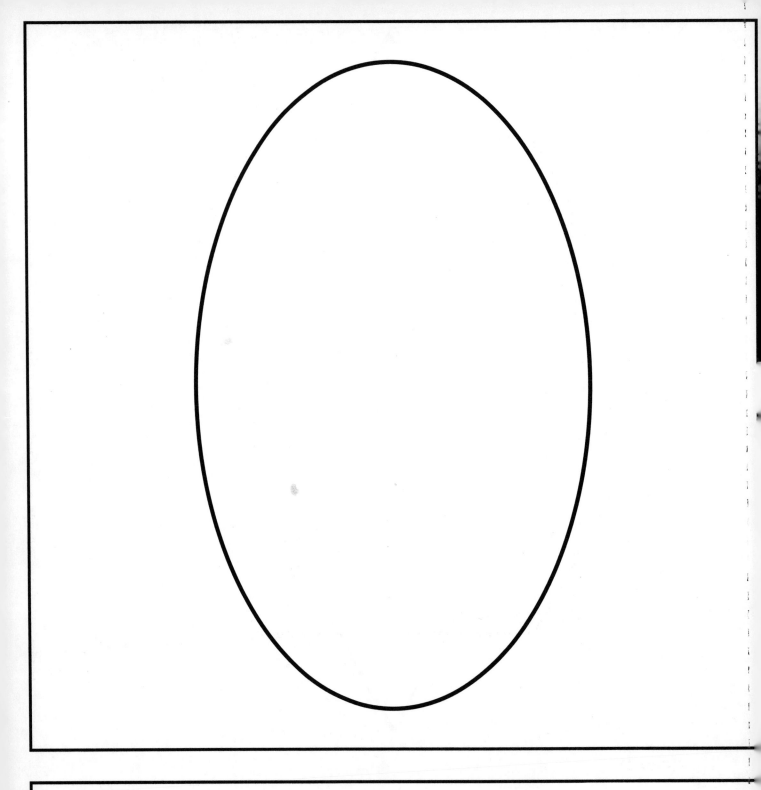

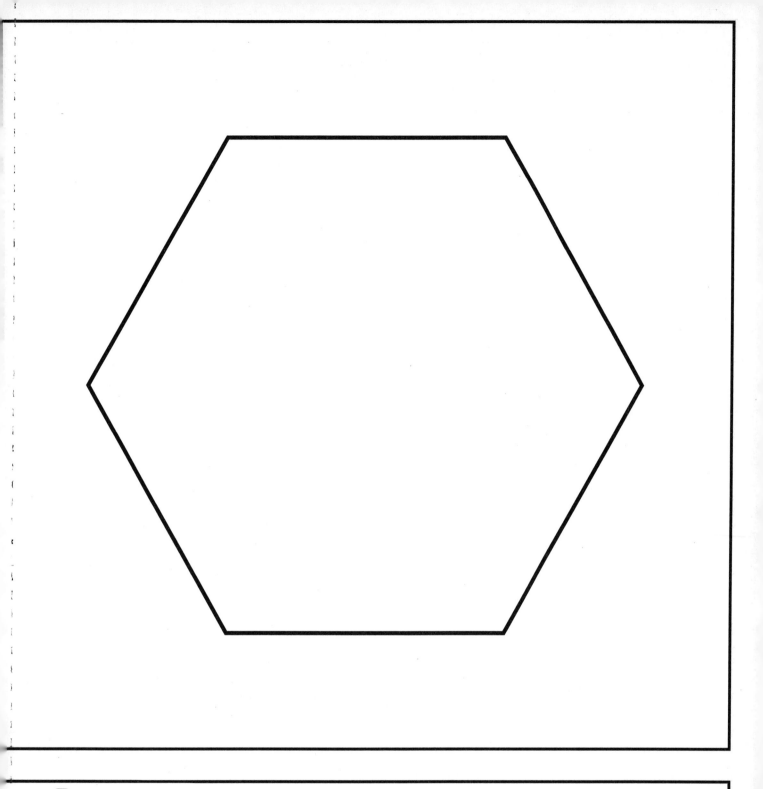

hexagon

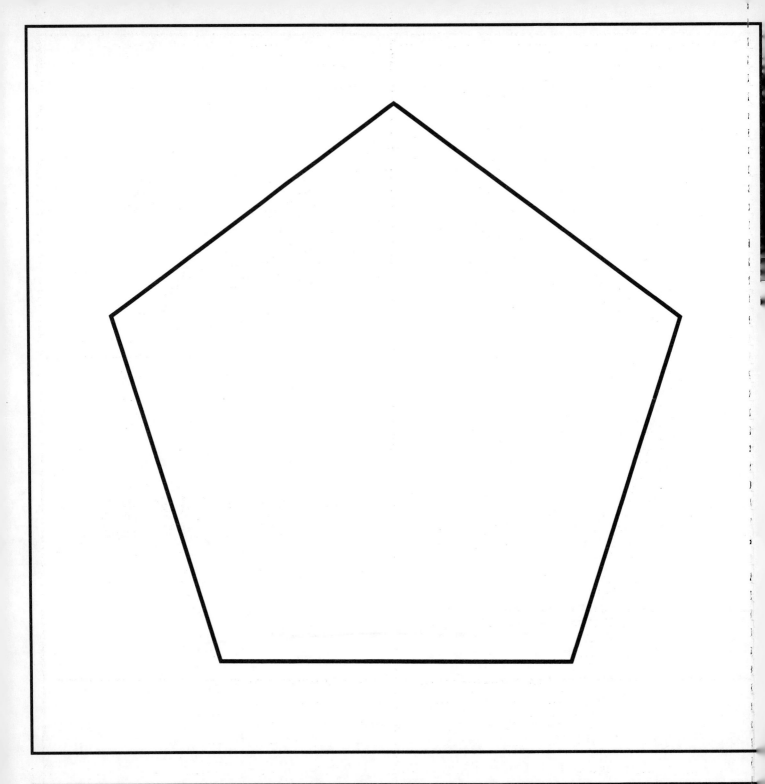

circle

square

triangle

153

rectangle

star

diamond

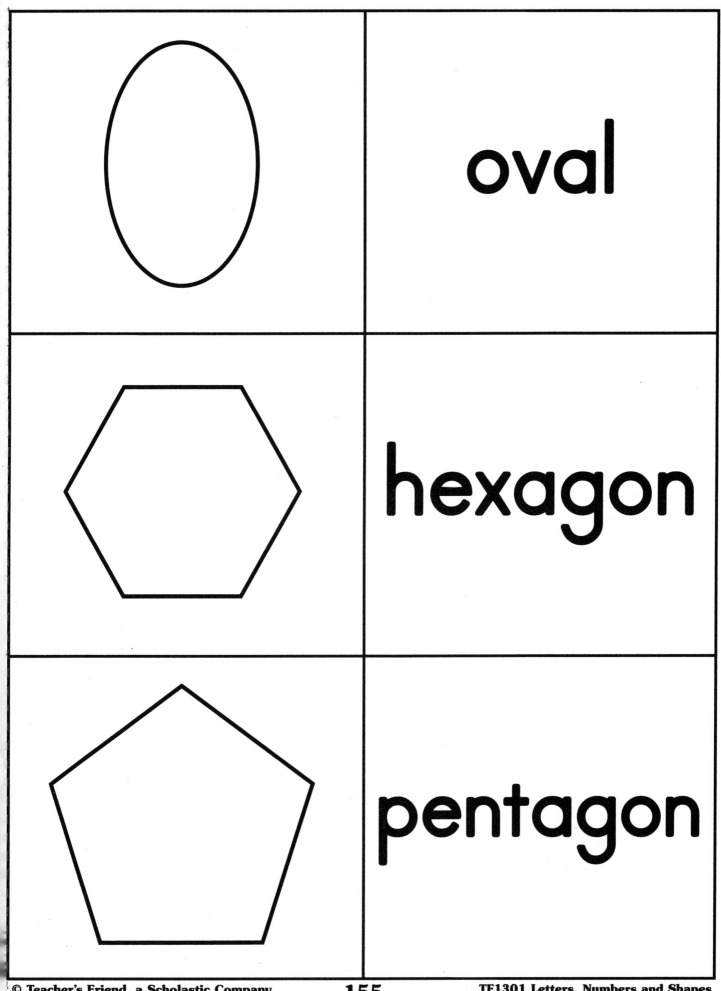

oval

hexagon

pentagon

Name _____

Color the shapes!
Color the circles red.
Color the squares blue.

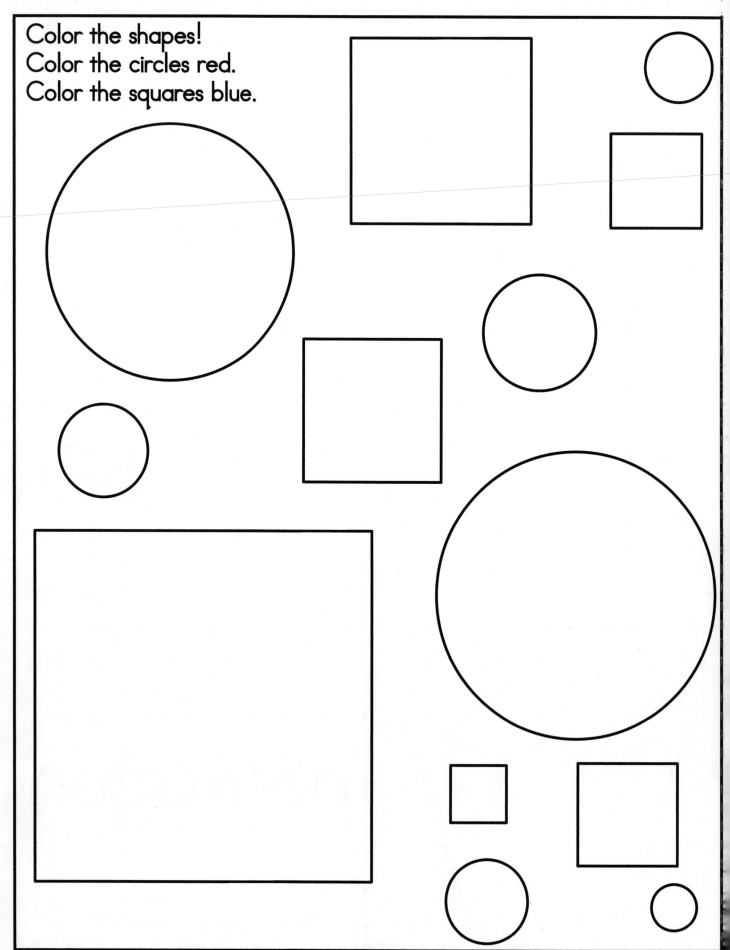

Name _____

Color the shapes!
Color the triangles orange.
Color the rectangles green.

Name _____

Color the shapes!
Color the diamonds purple.
Color the ovals yellow.

Name _____

Color the shapes!
Color the hexagons pink.
Color the pentagons brown.

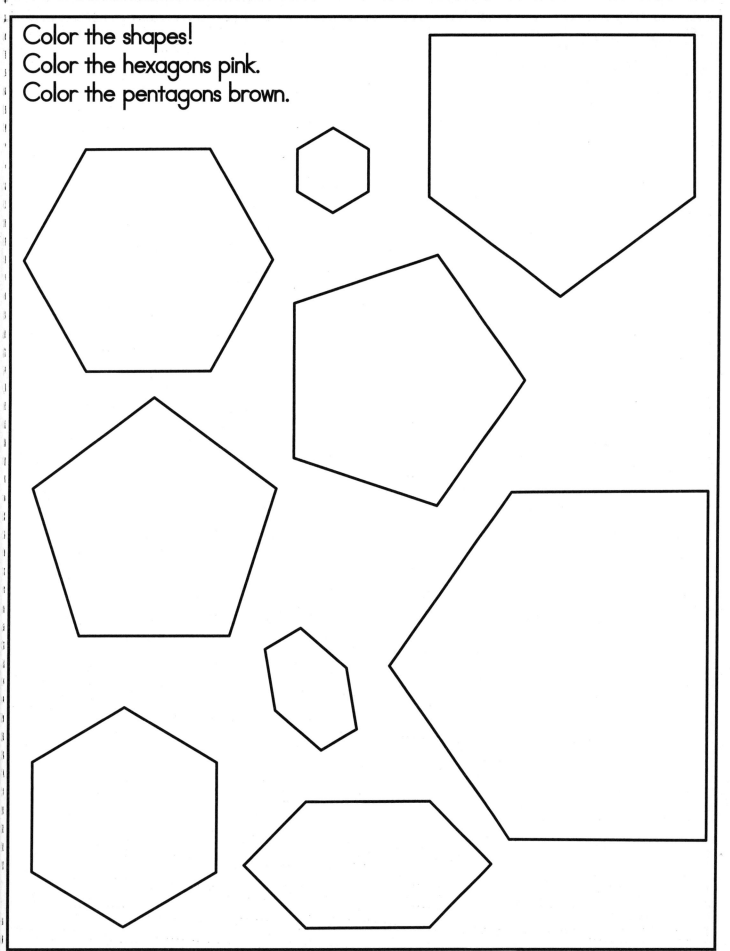

Count the stars. There are _____ stars.
Color the stars.

DIMES TIMES

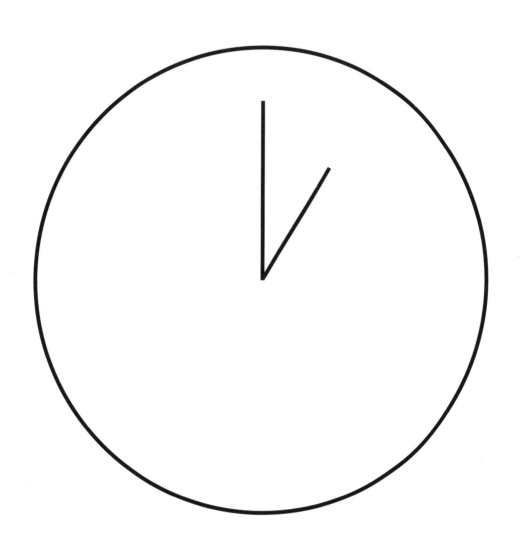

EMOTIONAL EATING